PUZZLES OF
FINANCE

Other books in the *Wiley Investment* series

Forthcoming:

PUZZLES OF FINANCE

Six Practical Problems and Their Remarkable Solutions

MARK P. KRITZMAN

John Wiley & Sons, Inc.
New York • Chichester • Weinheim • Brisbane • Singapore • Toronto

Published by John Wiley & Sons, Inc.
Published simultaneously in Canada.

This publication is designed to provide accurate and authoritative information
in regard to the subject matter covered. It is sold with the understanding that
the publisher is not engaged in rendering professional services. If professional
advice or other expert assistance is required, the services of a competent
professional person should be sought.

Library of Congress Cataloging-in-Publication Data:
Kritzman, Mark P.
   Puzzles of finance : six practical problems and their remarkable solutions
  / Mark Kritzman.
     p. cm.
  ISBN 0-471-24657-3 (cloth : alk)
   1. Investment analysis. 2. Finance, Personal. I. Title.
  HG4529.K75 2000
  332–dc21   99-055828

Printed in the United States of America.

10 9 8 7 6 5 4 3 2 1

FOREWORD

This book is an extraordinary combination of the elements of finance, common sense, wisdom, sparkling humor, shining clarity, and enviable originality. That is a potent blend by any standard of measurement. Longtime Kritzman-watchers, however, would anticipate nothing less.

I first came to know Mark Kritzman almost 20 years ago, in 1980, when he submitted an article to *The Journal of Portfolio Management,* of which I was then editor, under the title of "A Short-Term Approach to Asset Allocation." The paper provided a market-timing model that functioned within the constraints of investor utility and the longer term preferred asset mix. No one could read that article without sensing that here was a young man whose originality and analytical power would in time lead him to make a major contribution to the field. Indeed, this paper was only the first of a long series of articles by Kritzman that the *Journal* has had the honor to publish, covering a wide range of topics such as issues in performance measurement, currency management, and portfolio insurance. These, and Kritzman's other published materials, reveal the extent of his understanding of finance and his ability to translate difficult ideas into comprehensible language.

This new book is a further exploration into the many paths that Kritzman's inexhaustible intellectual curiosity has led him over the years. He rejoices in puzzles: He appreciates the fun that puzzles provide and leaps at the opportunity to use them for profound theoretical or practical generalization. He enjoys the challenge of finding complexity in what appears to be utmost simplicity and revealing simplicity in what appears to be hopelessly complex. He approaches the solutions to these puzzles like an explorer who penetrates into a deep forest with the confident knowledge that somewhere in the shadows he will find the light to lead him out at the other side.

The most important feature of Kritzman's chosen puzzles is their relevance. He is not just an intellectual acrobat who delights in conundrums. He spends the largest portion of his daily life on the firing line, managing money in some of the most sophisticated environments of the world of finance. After you have completed all the mental handsprings that Kritzman asks you to perform, you will find that the effort pays off in hard, practical insights that you can apply in your own daily responsibilities.

Kritzman has reserved one of the great treats of the book for the two final sections: his enlightening review of the basic concepts of finance and his invaluable glossary. These two sections alone are worth the price of admission, even though they appear at the end. Many readers, I suspect, would benefit from reading the book backward instead of in the conventional manner! I suggest that you begin with at least a look at the Primer, to make certain that you will be up to speed in working your way through the six chapters that precede it.

I cannot close this Foreword without adding that my long professional association with Mark Kritzman has developed into a rich personal friendship, embellished by a shared love for the state of Vermont, where we are neighbors during part of the year. I have leaned on him mercilessly when my own understanding of some matter was cloudy. It is gratifying to note that the generosity and steadfast integrity I have come to know so well shine through in the pages of this fine book.

PETER L. BERNSTEIN

PREFACE

This book presents six puzzles of finance and their solutions. These puzzles are interesting for two reasons. First, they address important financial concepts that continue to confound academics and investment professionals alike, and second, the intellectual paths that lead to their solutions are entertaining.

These puzzles are unlike some of the better-known finance puzzles, such as the dividend puzzle and the equity risk premium puzzle. The dividend puzzle questions why most companies pay dividends even though there is no apparent economic motivation to do so. The equity risk premium puzzle deals with the fact that the historical spread between stock returns and the return on a riskless asset is too large to accord with commonly accepted views about risk aversion. These two puzzles and others like them are technically unsolvable because they deal with human behavior. The best we can hope for are plausible conjectures supported by persuasive evidence. The puzzles presented in this book, by comparison, deal with logical and mathematical subtleties; hence the solutions I present are incontrovertible ... although I'm not always right.

Chapter 1 presents the first puzzle, which is called *Siegel's Paradox*. Jeremy Siegel, professor of finance at Wharton, drew attention to the mathematical fact that the expected value of the reciprocal of an exchange rate is greater than the reciprocal of the expected value of the exchange rate. This relationship implies that a particular percentage increase in a given currency corresponds to a smaller percentage decrease in the currency on the other side of the exchange rate. Does this mathematical truism have any economic relevance?

The next notion, *Likelihood of Loss,* is puzzling because, given the same information *and agreement* about a particular investment's expected return and risk and identical views about the process that generates its returns, the likelihood that this investment will produce a loss varies from hardly at all to very likely. The critical determinant is how we frame the question, a fact that is significantly under appreciated by most investment professionals and even world-class economists engaged in restructuring our social security system.

The puzzle *Time Diversification* is related to *Likelihood of Loss* but addresses a broader and more fundamental issue. How does time influence an investment's expected utility? The concept of utility, by itself, is intriguing and rich in intellectual history. The discovery of utility by the prominent mathematician, Daniel Bernoulli, solved the famous St. Petersburg Paradox, which was proposed by Daniel's cousin, Nicholas Bernoulli. *Time Diversification* embraces Bernoulli's description of utility and also has an amusing history. Paul A. Samuelson, America's first Nobel Prize winner in economics and arguably its greatest economist, challenged one of his MIT colleagues to a wager. His colleague's response inspired Samuelson to present the fallacy of large numbers, which provides the elegant solution to the *Time Diversification* puzzle.

Next is one of the more confounding and important puzzles of finance, *Why the Expected Return Is Not to Be Expected.*

Although the solution to this puzzle, once it is revealed, is astoundingly clear, intelligent and well-trained investment professionals continue to challenge its validity with annoying persistence.

The next puzzle, at first glance, seems rather straightforward, but on closer scrutiny, reveals surprising layers of complexity: *All Stocks Half the Time or Half Stocks All the Time?* This question appeared on the late Fischer Black's list of 50 questions that he would use to motivate discussions in his classes at MIT. More explicitly, Fischer posed the question: Are you better off by investing 100% of your savings in stocks 50% of the time and in a riskless asset the other 50% of the time, or by investing 50% of your savings in stocks and 50% in a riskless asset 100% of the time? It has been rumored that students would repeat Fischer's class even though his questions never changed. They returned because his answers changed. Paul A. Samuelson has since provided the dispositive answer to this intriguing puzzle.

The final and perhaps most profound puzzle is *The Irrelevance of Expected Return on Options.* The solution to this puzzle resulted in the famous Black-Scholes options pricing formula, which earned a Nobel Prize for Robert Merton and Myron Scholes. Sadly, Fischer Black passed away before the Nobel Committee officially recognized their achievement. This puzzle refers to the fact that the fair value of an option is invariant to the expected return of the underlying asset. The solution to this puzzle is remarkable for several reasons. Some of the greatest minds in science have contributed along the way to its ultimate solution, including no fewer than six Nobel laureates. Moreover, critical components of the solution are derived from seemingly unrelated fields, such as botany and thermodynamics.

I also include a primer on basic financial concepts and quantitative methods. Much of this material will be familiar, but no doubt, some of these topics had a soporific effect on you during your school days; thus, you may wish to refresh your memory before tackling the puzzles of finance. If you choose to ignore this material, however, it should not matter much. Each puzzle is presented in a self-contained manner with references to the relevant sections of the book.

Finally, I include a glossary so that you can quickly review the definitions of technical terms whose meanings may not be obvious from the context in which they are used.

MARK P. KRITZMAN

Cambridge, Massachusetts
March 2000

ACKNOWLEDGMENTS

I have been the beneficiary of many thoughtful discussions and comments for which I am deeply grateful. I would especially like to thank George Chow, Roger Clarke, Ken Froot, Chip Lowry, Alan Marcus, Paul O'Connell, Don Rich, Paul A. Samuelson, Edouard Stirling, and Jack Treynor. I owe an enormous debt of gratitude to Peter Bernstein. Some of these chapters were previewed in Peter's publication, *Economics and Portfolio Strategy*. Consequently, they were improved both substantively and stylistically by Peter's excellent editing. I am grateful to Roger Clarke, Don Rich, and Edouard Stirling, in particular for their careful reading of the entire manuscript, sparing me the embarrassment of several "thinkos" (that is, mistakes that are typed correctly). I would like to express my sincere appreciation to Mina Samuels, my editor at John Wiley & Sons. She exhibited a perfect balance between patience and suasion, and along the way she contributed many valuable ideas. My final thanks are for my wife, Elizabeth Gorman, who graciously indulged my absence as I completed this project and who has been a supportive partner in all things important to me.

M. P. K.

CONTENTS

xv

PUZZLES OF
FINANCE

CHAPTER 1

Siegel's Paradox

When the euro was introduced to the world on January 1, 1999, it was valued at 1.1800 dollars. By June 30th, it had depreciated 12.60% against the dollar to 1.0313. During the same six-month span, the dollar appreciated 14.42% against the euro from 0.8475 euros to 0.9697. Thus, the combined change in value of these two currencies was positive 1.82%. Is this number economically relevant or merely an artifact of currency accounting?

Exchange rates are annoying, not so much because they introduce uncertainty but because they are confusing. For example, each day the *New York Times* reports the change in the value of the euro and the yen on the front page of its business section. If the *Times* reports an increase in the euro, they mean that the euro appreciated, and it will cost Americans more for a pilgrimage to Lourdes. However, if the *Times* reports an increase in the yen, they really mean that the yen lost value relative to the dollar and Americans can afford more cameras. The reason for this annoying contradiction is that currency traders are a strange lot. They quote

1

the value of the euro as the number of dollars per euro, while they quote the value of the yen as the number of yen per dollar.

This little quirk in the way currency traders communicate is trivial, however, when compared to the confusion introduced by exchange rate arithmetic. For example, if the dollar were to rise 25% against the euro, I could buy 25% more French wine. Of course, my friend Edouard in France wouldn't be so happy, because he prefers wine from Napa Valley. But he would not be disadvantaged by the exchange rate change to the same extent that I benefit from it. Given a 25% increase in the dollar, the euro only decreases 20% against the dollar (1/1.25 = 0.80). Can it be true that Edouard and I are collectively better off?

This asymmetry in exchange rate changes is a feature of *Siegel's paradox*. Although most investors find Siegel's paradox bothersome because it complicates financial analysis, I take the view that we should be grateful for the opportunity it affords us to consume more wine. But before I explain how we can consume more wine, let me describe Siegel's paradox a little more precisely.

Siegel's paradox refers to the mathematical fact that the expectation of the reciprocal of an exchange rate is greater than the reciprocal of the expectation of the exchange rate. If we let E represent the expectation and S represent the exchange rate, then we can write Siegel's paradox as:

$$E\left(\frac{1}{S}\right) > \frac{1}{\left[E(S)\right]} \qquad (1.1)$$

Suppose, for example, that the euro is currently valued at 1.0600 dollars and we expect it will either increase 25% to

Table 1.1 Siegel's paradox.

	Dollars per Euro	Euros per Dollar
Current exchange rate	1.0600	0.9434
Euro appreciates 25%	1.3250	0.7547
Euro depreciates 25%	0.7950	1.2579
Expected value	1.0600	
Expected value of reciprocal		*1.0063*
Reciprocal of expected value	*0.9434*	

1.3250 dollars or depreciate 25% to 0.7950 dollars with equal probability. The expectation of the reciprocal of these potential outcomes is 1.0063 euros. If the euro rises 25%, the dollar falls to 0.7547 euros (1/1.3250), and if the euro falls 25%, the dollar rises to 1.2579 euros (1/0.7950). The expectation of these two outcomes equals 0.7547 times 50% plus 1.2579 times 50%, which is 1.0063.

The reciprocal of the expectation of the euro, however, equals only 0.9434. Because the euro has an equal chance of increasing to 1.3250 or decreasing to 0.7950, its expectation is 1.0600 and the reciprocal of this value is 0.9434. This relationship is presented in Table 1.1.

This feature of reciprocal relationships is known as Jensen's inequality.[1] Jeremy Siegel showed that as a result of Jensen's inequality, the currency forward rate cannot be an unbiased estimate of the future spot rate because an expected increase in one exchange rate implies an expected

---

[1] Jensen's inequality is discussed by C. Radhakrishna Rao in *Linear Statistical Inferences and Its Applications* (New York: John Wiley & Sons, 1965), p. 46.

decrease of smaller magnitude in its reciprocal.[2] Therefore, even if expected changes in the spot rate are distributed symmetrically around the forward rate from the perspective of one investor, Siegel's paradox guarantees that the forward rate will be biased from the perspective of the investor on the other side of the exchange rate. To understand why the forward rate must be biased, let's review covered and uncovered interest arbitrage.

COVERED INTEREST ARBITRAGE

Covered interest arbitrage describes the economic forces that relate the difference between the domestic and foreign interest rate to the difference between the spot exchange rate and the forward exchange rate. The spot rate is the rate at which currencies are exchanged at the present time as opposed to a future date. By contrast, the forward rate is a previously agreed on rate at which currencies are exchanged on a future date. Covered interest arbitrage ensures that a currency's forward rate will equal its spot rate multiplied by the ratio of one plus the domestic interest rate to one plus the foreign interest rate, as shown:

$$F = S \times \frac{\left(1 + R_d\right)}{\left(1 + R_f\right)}$$

[2] Jeremy J. Siegel, "Risk, Interest Rates, and the Forward Exchange," *Quarterly Journal of Economics* (February 1975), pp. 303–309.

where F = Forward exchange rate (domestic units per foreign unit)

S = Spot exchange rate (domestic units per foreign unit)

R_d = Domestic interest rate

R_f = Foreign interest rate

In liquid markets, this relationship must hold; otherwise arbitrageurs would earn riskless profits. Consider the following example: Suppose one-year interest rates in the United States are 5%, while one-year rates in the United Kingdom are 8%. Further, suppose that one pound can be exchanged in the spot market for 1.6000 dollars. It must follow that the one-year forward rate to exchange pounds for dollars equals 1.5556 (1.6000 × 1.05/1.08). To see why this relationship must hold, imagine that a dealer agrees to exchange pounds for dollars one year hence at a rate of 1.5700 instead of 1.5556. An arbitrageur could borrow $1,600,000 in the United States at 5%, convert the dollars to 1,000,000 pounds, lend the pounds at 8%, and sell a forward contract to hedge the loan. The forward contract must be sufficient to cover the principal amount of the loan as well as the interest it generates; thus the arbitrageur would sell pounds forward in an amount equal to $1,695,600 (1,000,000 × 1.08 × 1.5700). These transactions would produce a riskless profit of $15,600 regardless of the level of the spot rate one year from now. Table 1.2 illustrates this point by assuming the spot rate either increases 10% to 1.7600 or falls 10% to 1.4400.

The gain or loss on the principal amount of the loan is calculated by subtracting the initial dollar value of the loan (1.6000 × 1,000,000) from the dollar value of the loan when it matures (1.7600 × 1,000,000 or 1.4400 × 1,000,000). The

Table 1.2 Arbitrage profits when the forward rate is too high.

Cash Flows	Spot Rate Increases to 1.7600 ($)	Spot Rate Decreases to 1.4400 ($)
Interest cost from borrowing $1,600,000 at 5%	−80,000	−80,000
Gain or loss on principal from change in spot rate	160,000	−160,000
Interest received after change in spot rate	140,800	115,200
Gain or loss from short forward position (−$1,080,000 × 1.5700)	−205,200	140,400
Net profit	15,600	15,600

dollar value of the interest received is equal to the 80,000 pounds (1,000,000 × 8%) multiplied by either 1.7600 or 1.4400. The gain or loss on the short forward position used to hedge the loan arises from closing the position by repurchasing the 1,080,000 pounds at the exchange rate prevailing when the loan matures, which again is either 1.7600 or 1.4400. The ending exchange rate doesn't matter, however. The profit will always equal $15,600 given these transactions as long as the forward rate equals 1.5700. If it were higher, an arbitrageur could earn greater profits. If the forward exchange rate, given the spot rate and interest rates in this example, were lower than 1.5556, then an arbitrageur could earn riskless profits by reversing these transactions. It is only when the forward rate equals 1.5556 precisely that an arbitrageur is unable to profit without incurring risk, because the forward discount exactly offsets the interest rate advantage of lending in the United Kingdom. This condition is referred to as *covered interest arbitrage,* which is illustrated in Table 1.3.

Table 1.3 Covered interest arbitrage.

Cash Flows	Spot Rate Increases to 1.7600 ($)	Spot Rate Decreases to 1.4400 ($)
Interest cost from borrowing $1,600,000 at 5%	−80,000	−80,000
Gain or loss on principal from change in spot rate	160,000	−160,000
Interest received after change in spot rate	140,800	115,200
Gain or loss from short forward position (−$1,080,000 × 1.5556)	−220,800	124,800
Net profit	0	0

UNCOVERED INTEREST ARBITRAGE

Uncovered interest arbitrage is the notion that, *on average,* the spot rate will move to the forward rate, which implies that arbitrageurs do not profit, *on average,* by borrowing in low interest rate countries and lending in high interest rate countries, even if they choose not to hedge these transactions. In essence, uncovered interest arbitrage holds that the forward rate is an unbiased estimate of the future spot rate.

Consider, for example, an arbitrageur who borrows $1,600,000 in the United States at 5%, converts these dollars to 1,000,000 pounds, and lends them at 8% in the United Kingdom. Rather than selling a forward contract to hedge the loan in the United Kingdom, however, the arbitrageur accepts the risk that the pound might depreciate.[3] If the

---

[3] This notion is somewhat oxymoronic because arbitrageurs by definition do not accept risk.

forward exchange rate is an unbiased estimate of the future spot rate, then on average these transactions should not generate profits. In some instances, the spot rate will depreciate by more than the forward discount, in which case the arbitrageur will suffer losses, and in other instances the spot rate will fall by less than the forward discount or even increase, which would produce a gain for the arbitrageur. On balance, however, these gains and losses would cancel out if the forward rate is the mean of the distribution of future spot rates. This condition is called *uncovered interest arbitrage,* because the foreign loan is not covered by a hedge.

Table 1.4 shows that the gain and loss cancel each other out when the spot rate increases or decreases by 10% from the forward rate. In this example, the gain or loss on the principal comes from receiving $1,711,111 (1.7111 × 1,000,000) or $1,400,000 (1.4000 × 1,000,000) at maturity compared to the initial dollar value of the loan of $1,600,000. The dollar value of the interest similarly is calculated by multiplying the 80,000 pounds by 1.7111 and by

Table 1.4 Uncovered interest arbitrage when the spot rate changes 10% from the forward rate.

Cash Flows	Spot Rate Increases to 1.7111 ($)	Spot Rate Decreases to 1.4000 ($)
Interest cost from borrowing $1,600,000 at 5%	−80,000	−80,000
Gain or loss on principal from change in spot rate	111,111	−200,000
Interest received after change in spot rate	136,889	112,000
Net profit	168,000	−168,000

1.4000. This result will prevail regardless of the magnitude of the changes in the spot rate provided they are symmetric around the forward rate, *from the perspective of the U.S. investor.*

It is not necessarily the case, however, that the forward rate is an unbiased estimate of the future spot rate. It may be that spot rate changes are centered on the current spot rate rather than the forward rate. In this case, the forward rate would be a biased estimate of the future spot rate. However, even if changes in the spot rate are distributed symmetrically around the forward rate from the perspective of one investor, Siegel's paradox guarantees that the forward rate will be biased from the perspective of the investor on the other side of the exchange rate. In the previous example, the forward rate is the unbiased estimate of the future spot rate from the perspective of the U.S. investor. Let's now examine the implication of this estimate from the perspective of the U.K. investor (Table 1.5).

If the dollar appreciates to 1.7111, the pound depreciates to 0.5844 (1/1.7111), and if it falls to 1.4000, the pound rises

Table 1.5 Uncovered interest arbitrage from the United Kingdom perspective.

Cash Flows	Spot Rate Decreases to 0.5844 (£)	Spot Rate Increases to 0.7143 (£)
Interest cost from borrowing $1,600,000 at 5%	−46,753	−57,143
Gain or loss on principal from change in spot rate	64,935	−142,857
Interest received after change in spot rate	80,000	80,000
Net profit	98,182	−120,000

to 0.7143 (1/1.4000). Note that these changes are not symmetric around the current forward rate of 0.6429 (1/1.5556) from the U.K. perspective. Whereas 0.5844 is 9.10% below the forward rate, 0.7143 is 11.10% above it; hence the forward rate from the U.K. perspective is a biased estimate of the distribution of future spot rates. This bias is a mathematical consequence of the bilateral nature of exchange rates. Not only is uncovered interest arbitrage untrue bilaterally. It's impossible!

IS SIEGEL'S PARADOX ECONOMICALLY RELEVANT?

The mathematical truth of Siegel's paradox is incontrovertible, but does it have any economic relevance? In other words, does it apply to realized exchange rate changes as well as to expectations and, if it does generate realized gains, is it possible to spend these gains to produce incremental welfare? To address these questions, let's return to the question I posed at the outset. Can Edouard and I drink more wine as a consequence of asymmetry of exchange rate changes? If so, we might be inclined to conclude that Siegel's paradox is indeed economically relevant or, at the very least, gastronomically interesting.

Suppose that I have an annual wine budget of 7,500 dollars, and that Edouard spends an equal amount of euros on wine each year. Let's also suppose that the dollar and the euro are at parity and that the average price of a bottle of wine in the United States is 30 dollars and in France 30 euros. With these assumptions, we can each buy 250 bottles of wine. I simply go to my favorite wine purveyor in the

United States and Edouard does the same in France, and we collectively purchase 500 bottles of wine.

Here is how we exploit Siegel's paradox to purchase more wine. We begin by converting our wine budgets. I convert my 7,500 dollar wine budget to 7,500 euros, and Edouard converts his 7,500 euro wine budget to 7,500 dollars. Then we wait for the exchange rate to change. Suppose the euro rises to 1.25 dollars. I reconvert my 7,500 euros to 9,375 dollars, and purchase 312½ bottles of wine. At the same time, Edouard reconverts his 7,500 dollars to 6,000 euros (1/1.25 × 7,500) and purchases 200 bottles of wine. Thus we end up with 512½ bottles of wine to split between us rather than 500 bottles had we not converted our currencies. The 25% gain in the value of the euro flows directly to the quantity of wine that can be purchased as does the 20% devaluation of the dollar.

If, instead, the dollar rises 25% against the euro, we still end up with 12½ additional bottles of wine. This time Edouard purchases 312½ bottles by reconverting his 7,500 dollars to 9,375 euros, and I purchase 200 bottles by reconverting my 7,500 euros to 6000 dollars.[4]

Based on this example, the asymmetry of exchange rate changes associated with Siegel's paradox conveys a tangible economic benefit. We can repeat this strategy over and over again to purchase more wine than we could had we not converted our currencies. This will be true regardless of which direction the exchange rate moves, as long as it deviates from the exchange rate that prevailed when the price of wine was

---

[4] This example ignores a variety of real world complexities. For example, it ignores interest rates and transportation costs. Nonetheless, the absence of these details does not alter the conclusion qualitatively.

set and wine prices stay constant or change by less than the amount required to offset the exchange rate change. Table 1.6 compares the quantity of wine we could purchase by exploiting this asymmetry to the quantity that we could otherwise purchase.

Table 1.6 reveals that as long as the prevailing exchange rate differs from the initial exchange rate, it is possible to purchase more wine if we convert our currencies prior to an exchange rate change and then reconvert them after an exchange rate change. Does this economic advantage extend to the economy as a whole? If so, there are some interesting implications.

Table 1.6 Quantity of wine as an indication of the economic relevance of Siegel's paradox.

	Before Rate Change	Euro Appreciates	Dollar Appreciates
Dollars per euro	1.00	1.25	0.80
Euros per dollar	1.00	0.80	1.25
Mark's wine budget in U.S. dollars	7,500	7,500	7,500
Edouard's wine budget in euros	7,500	7,500	7,500
Mark's wine budget in euros	7,500	6,000	9,375
Edouard's wine budget in U.S. dollars	7,500	9,375	6,000
Price of wine in U.S. dollars	30.00	30.00	30.00
Price of wine in euros	30.00	30.00	30.00
Wine purchased without exchanging currencies	500.00	500.00	500.00
Wine purchased by exchanging currencies	500.00	512.50	512.50

For example, consider the decision to establish the euro as Europe's single currency. If the gains associated with Siegel's paradox could be extended to the entire European community, then the euro was a big mistake by at least one measure. By eliminating exchange rate fluctuations, the European

---

The Paradox of the Lost Dollar

Siegel's paradox shows how we can consume more wine by exchanging money. The paradox of the lost dollar shows how we can lose money by consuming wine.

Suppose that Edouard, JF (another wine loving friend), and I meet for drinks at our favorite wine bar. After having a few glasses of wine, we are presented with a bill for 30 dollars, service compris. We each give the waiter 10 dollars. The waiter takes the 30 dollars and our bill to the cashier, who notices an error in the addition. The cashier points out to the waiter that we should have been charged only 25 dollars and gives the waiter 5 dollars to return to us. Unfortunately, the waiter is not particularly honest or perhaps is too lazy to divide 3 into 5. Instead he keeps 2 dollars and gives back to each of us only 1 dollar. Thus instead of paying 10 dollars each, we paid 9 dollars each, which is 27 dollars altogether. Given that the waiter kept only 2 dollars, what happened to the other dollar from the original 30 dollars?

Unlike Siegel's paradox, the paradox of the lost dollar is a trick question.

Answer: Edouard, JF, and I paid 25 dollars, not 27 dollars. The waiter returned 3 dollars and kept 2 dollars, which accounts for the original 30 dollars.

community eliminated the economic gains that result from asymmetry of exchange rate changes. Indeed, as a counterexample, the United States should convert the dollar to 50 separate state currencies, so that these exchange rate gains could be applied to reduce the national debt, lower taxes, wage war, or increase spending on social programs.

But alas, the notion that asymmetry of exchange rate changes generates economic gains for everyone is fanciful. Although this asymmetry might convey real economic benefits to some individuals, it cannot benefit everyone at the same time. The reason it succeeds in generating a real economic gain for Edouard and myself in the wine example is because the price of wine in both countries remains constant. If wine prices adjust to exchange rate changes, then we could not gain economically from asymmetry of exchange rate changes. In fact, the strategy I contrived to exploit Siegel's paradox does not maximize the quantity of wine we could purchase. To maximize the quantity of wine, Edouard and I would simply pool our funds and purchase all of the wine in the country whose currency depreciated.

SIEGEL'S PARADOX AND PURCHASING POWER PARITY

If wine prices adjust to exchange rate changes, we do not gain economically from asymmetry of exchange rate changes. For example, suppose we pool our funds to purchase something whose price responds immediately and continuously to exchange rate fluctuations, such as another currency. Table 1.7

Table 1.7 Quantity of Aussie dollars as an indication of the economic irrelevance of Siegel's paradox.

	Before Rate Change	Euro Appreciates	Dollar Appreciates
Dollars per euro	1.00	1.25	0.80
Euros per dollar	1.00	0.80	1.25
Mark's Aussie dollar budget in U.S. dollars	7,500	7,500	7,500
Edouard's Aussie dollar budget in euros	7,500	7,500	7,500
Mark's Aussie dollar budget in euros	7,500	6,000	9,375
Edouard's Aussie dollar budget in U.S. dollars	7,500	9,375	6,000
Price of Aussie dollar in U.S. dollars	0.75	0.75	0.75
Price of Aussie dollar in euros	0.75	0.60	0.94
Aussie dollars purchased without exchanging currencies	20,000.00	22,500.00	18,000.00
Aussie dollars purchased by exchanging currencies	20,000.00	22,500.00	18,000.00

reveals that the asymmetry of exchange rate changes associated with Siegel's paradox does not permit gains if we use our funds to purchase the Australian dollar, because it tracks exchange rate fluctuations precisely.

Whether or not Edouard and I exchange our respective currencies to purchase Aussie dollars is immaterial. Collectively, we will purchase the same quantity of Aussie dollars, which reveals that Siegel's paradox does not permit economic gains if purchasing power parity holds.

Purchasing power parity is the principle that exchange rates adjust so that the cost of similar goods and services remains the same in all countries, which implies that exchange rate changes offset relative inflation rates. There is

---

Currency Cross Rates

A currency cross rate is the implied exchange rate between two currencies that is derived from their respective exchange rates with a third currency. For example, suppose the exchange rate between the U.S. dollar and the euro is 1.0500 dollars per euro and that the exchange rate between the U.S. dollar and the Aussie dollar is 0.7500 U.S. dollars per Aussie dollar. These two relationships imply that the cross rate between the euro and the Aussie dollar is 0.7143 euros per Aussie dollar.

The euros per Aussie dollar cross rate is found by dividing the U.S. dollars per Aussie dollar exchange rate of 0.7500 by the U.S. dollars per euro exchange rate of 1.0500. The reciprocal of this value expresses the cross rate as Aussie dollars per euro, which equals 1.4000. This value can also be found by dividing the euros per U.S. dollars exchange rate, which equals 0.9524 (1/1.0500), by the Aussie dollars per U.S. dollar exchange rate 1.3333 (1/0.7500).

The extraordinary liquidity of currency markets renders arbitrage virtually costless and effortless and thus ensures that currency cross rates track their purchasing power parity value.

---

an extensive literature about whether or not purchasing power parity holds, and if not, why.[5] Violations of purchasing power parity occur and may persist for extended periods because consumer preferences differ from country to country and because there are impediments to trade. In the long run, however, it is reasonable to expect that arbitrage of goods and services will force exchange rates and prices to converge.

The Aussie dollar example reveals that it is not possible to generate real gains from asymmetry of exchange rate changes globally. The apparent monetary gain is a subtle illusion that arises from mixing measurement units. If we substitute real goods for currencies, the illusion becomes transparent.

Suppose Edouard has 100 bottles of red wine and I have 100 bottles of white wine. If the exchange rate shifts from one bottle of red wine for one bottle of white wine to 1½ bottles of red wine for one bottle of white wine, the monetary value of these 200 bottles of wine increases to 217 bottles of wine. The monetary (white wine) value of Edouard's red wine declines to 67 bottles of white wine (1/1.5), while the monetary (red wine) value of my white wine increases to 150 bottles of red wine. Yet the physical quantity of wine remains 200 bottles (Table 1.8).

This apparent increase in the monetary value of wine is identical to the apparent increase in collective currency values following an exchange rate shift when viewed simultaneously from both base currencies. It's an illusion.

---

[5] For an authoritative discussion of purchasing power parity, see Paul O'Connell, "The Overvaluation of Purchasing Power Parity," *Journal of International Economics,* vol. 44 (1998), pp. 1–19.

Table 1.8   The illusion of Siegel's paradox exposed.

Units and Value of Wine	Before Rate Change	White Wine Appreciates
Units of white wine per units of red wine	1.00	1.50
Units of red wine per units of white wine	1.00	0.67
Bottles of white wine	100	100
Bottles of red wine	100	100
White wine monetized in units of red wine	100	67
Red wine monetized in units of white wine	100	150
Total bottles of wine	200	200
Total monetary units of wine	200	217

EXCHANGE RATE CHANGES AND AGGREGATE UTILITY[6]

Although it is easy to demonstrate that exchange rate changes do not directly generate an increase in goods and services, it is less clear whether or not exchange rate volatility affects aggregate utility in a predictable way. Utility measures the amount of satisfaction we derive from consumption of goods and services.[7] A commonly invoked function relating utility to the quantity of goods and services is the Cobb-Douglas utility function, which holds that the fraction of our income we spend on a particular good relative to a competing good equals the relative utility we derive from that good.

If we let I_W equal the fraction of our income spent on white wine and I_R equal the fraction of our income spent on

---

[6] I thank Paul O'Connell for sharing these ideas with me and for producing the results in Table 1.9.

[7] The concept of utility is discussed in greater detail in Chapter 3, pp. 52–53.

red wine, then the utility we derive from wine consumption according to the Cobb-Douglas utility function equals:

$$U = (I_W)^a \times (I_R)^b$$

where a and b represent the relative satisfaction we derive from consumption of white and red wine, respectively.

Further, let's set the price of wine to equal $(a/b) \times (R/W)$, where R and W equal the quantity of red and white wine. This description of the price of wine reflects the relative scarcity of red and white wine arising from differences in preferences and endowments.

If we alter our relative preference or endowment of red and white wine, we can observe the effect of these changes on both the exchange rate and aggregate utility. Table 1.9 indicates that there is no causal relationship between exchange rate changes and aggregate utility. Depending on shifts in our preference for red and white wine and adjustments to our endowments of red and white wine, exchange rate changes may be associated with no change, a symmetric change, or an asymmetric change in aggregate utility.

What does this mean? Simply put, exchange rate changes do not affect aggregate utility. Rather, exchange rates and aggregate utility are both consequences of real changes in the economy, arising from shifts in preferences and endowments.

THE BOTTOM LINE

- Siegel's paradox refers to the mathematical fact that the expected value of the reciprocal of an exchange rate is greater than the reciprocal of the expected value

Table 1.9 Aggregate utility as a function of preference and endowment shifts.

Mark's Preference		Mark's White Wine	Edouard's Preference		Edouard's Red Wine		Mark's	Edouard's	Aggregate
White Wine	Red Wine	Endowment	White Wine	Red Wine	Endowment	Price	Utility	Utility	Utility
0.60	0.40	100.00	0.60	0.40	100.00	1.50	60.00	40.00	100.00
0.50	0.50	100.00	0.50	0.50	100.00	1.00	50.00	50.00	100.00
0.40	0.60	100.00	0.40	0.60	100.00	0.67	40.00	60.00	100.00
0.54	0.36	100.00	0.54	0.36	100.00	1.50	39.84	27.66	67.50
0.45	0.45	100.00	0.45	0.45	100.00	1.00	33.81	33.81	67.62
0.36	0.54	100.00	0.36	0.54	100.00	0.67	27.66	39.84	67.50
0.54	0.36	100.00	0.54	0.36	100.00	1.50	39.84	27.66	67.50
0.36	0.36	100.00	0.36	0.36	100.00	1.00	16.72	16.72	33.44
0.24	0.36	100.00	0.24	0.36	100.00	0.67	9.15	11.67	20.81
0.50	0.50	150.00	0.50	0.50	100.00	0.67	61.24	61.24	122.47
0.50	0.50	100.00	0.50	0.50	100.00	1.00	50.00	50.00	100.00
0.50	0.50	66.67	0.50	0.50	100.00	1.50	40.82	40.82	81.65

of the exchange rate. This relationship implies that a given increase in an exchange rate from the perspective of one investor corresponds to a smaller decrease from the perspective of the investor on the other side of the exchange rate.

- It is possible for a subset of investors to generate economic gains for themselves as a consequence of asymmetry of exchange rate changes, together with violation of purchasing power parity, but there are more effective ways to exploit failure of purchasing power parity.

- If purchasing power parity holds such that exchange rate changes offset price changes, it is not possible to benefit from asymmetry of exchange rate changes.

- The appearance of a combined monetary gain from asymmetry of exchange rate changes is an illusion arising from the combination of different measurement units. The apparent monetary gain does not translate into a real gain globally.

- Exchange rate changes are not causally related to changes in the aggregate utility of an economy. Both exchange rate volatility and aggregate utility are consequences of real changes in the economy such as shifts in preferences and endowments.

CHAPTER 2

Likelihood of Loss

> During the past 73 years, the U.S. stock market had an average annual return of 13.17% and a standard deviation of 20.26%. Based on this history, what is the likelihood you will lose 10% or more over a 10-year horizon if you invest in the stock market?
>
> (A) 0.03%   (B) 77.06%
>
> Both answers are correct, as are many values in between 0.03% and 77.06%.

Financial loss impairs our ability to consume, borrow, save, sustain a business, sustain our self-esteem, and in some cases, sustain our spouse or partner and children. It adversely affects our material and emotional well-being. The same is true for institutions and governments. Corporations that experience financial loss have more trouble raising capital and have fewer funds to invest in research and development. Endowment funds and foundations have less capital to support their spending programs. Financial loss limits a government's ability to provide services for its citizens and to defend itself. There is nothing puzzling about the seriousness of financial loss. Rather, what we often find puzzling is how to evaluate the likelihood of loss. We are puzzled because subtle variations in a problem often lead to dramatic changes in the likelihood of loss. If we fail to account properly for these subtle variations, we might misperceive our exposure to risk.

We begin with a simple question: What is the likelihood that an investment in the stock market will generate a particular loss during a single period? We answer this question with empirical methods by reviewing the investment's historical performance.

We then extend these principles to develop a theoretical framework for assessing the likelihood of loss. We review the central limit theorem and learn why it leads to the famous normal distribution. We then explore the properties of the normal distribution and learn how it is used to assess the likelihood of loss.

Next we consider variations to our original question that can be answered analytically; that is, by solving a formula:

- What is the likelihood of a particular loss *on average* over several periods?

- What is the likelihood of a particular loss *cumulatively* over several periods?

- What is the likelihood of a particular loss *in at least one* of the next several periods?

- What is the likelihood that *at any point* during our investment horizon, our investment will penetrate a particular threshold?

Finally, we consider a variation to our original question, but one that we cannot easily solve with a formula. Instead, we invoke numerical methods to deal with a problem called path dependency. What is the likelihood of penetrating a particular threshold on two or more consecutive calendar year-ends?

We discover that the likelihood of a particular loss legitimately ranges from 0.03% to 77.06% given identical assumptions about an investment's expected return and risk, but with slight variations in the construction of the question.

LIKELIHOOD OF A PARTICULAR LOSS IN ANY SINGLE PERIOD

Suppose we base our analysis on the stock market's annual returns from 1926 through 1998. What is the likelihood that an investment in the stock market will result in a loss of 10% or more? One way to assess the likelihood of this event is to count the number of years in which the stock market's return was −10% or less and to divide it by 73, the number of years in the sample. It turns out that the stock market lost 10% or more in 8 of the years since 1926 (1930, 1931, 1937, 1941, 1957, 1966, 1973, and 1974), which is 10.96% of the years. This value is called the relative frequency, and it is a reasonable approximation of the likelihood of experiencing a particular result if we believe our sample of returns is representative of the future. In fact, statisticians often rearrange data into a frequency distribution (also called a histogram) to show the relative frequency of a variety of outcomes. A frequency distribution assigns each of the returns to intervals of equal magnitude and plots the fraction of returns that is assigned to each interval. Figure 2.1 presents a frequency distribution for return intervals of 10%, starting at −50%.

This frequency distribution of historical stock market annual returns shows that one return was less than −40%, one return was between −40% and −30%, two returns were between −30% and −20%, and four returns were between −20% and −10%, for a total of eight returns below −10%. Thus we estimate the likelihood of experiencing a return less than −10% to equal 8/73 or 10.96%. We can also estimate the likelihood of experiencing a return above 10% by summing the percentages in all of the intervals to the right of 10%. Similarly, we can estimate the likelihood of experiencing returns that fall between two values by summing the percentages of the intervals between the values.

The precision of this approach improves as we increase the number of observations and the frequency with which

Figure 2.1 Frequency distribution of stock returns.

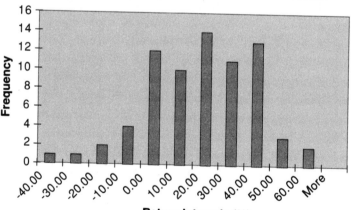

Figure 2.2 Empirical and theoretical distribution of stock returns.

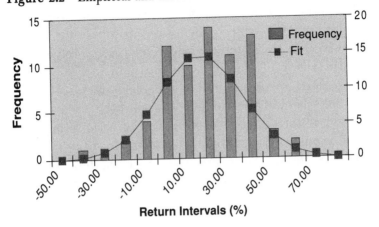

we measure returns. Indeed, if we had a very large number of returns that were independent and from the same underlying distribution, then the continuous analogues of these returns would be distributed normally. Figure 2.2 contrasts a normal distribution based on the mean and standard deviation of the historical returns with the frequency distribution of the returns.

The normal distribution is one of the most profound and ubiquitous results in science. It describes such diverse natural phenomena as the clustering of stars, the interval of time between eruptions of Old Faithful, and the movement of pollen particles suspended in fluid when it is agitated. In fact, it is this latter phenomenon that gave rise to the term Brownian motion, which is the stochastic process that generates a normal distribution.[1]

---

[1] See Chapter 6 for a more detailed discussion of Brownian motion and its discovery.

The central limit theorem explains why so many random variables produce normal distributions or in the case of periodic investment returns, lognormal distributions. (I will shortly explain the difference between a normal and lognormal distribution.) It states that the distribution of the sum or average of independent random variables, which are not individually normally distributed, will approach a normal distribution if the number of variables is large enough. A formal proof of this theorem is presented in many statistics books. For those who demand less rigor, the following example should provide adequate evidence of the veracity of the central limit theorem.

Figure 2.3 shows the theoretical distribution of the values resulting from the toss of a fair die, for which all six potential outcomes have an equal probability of occurrence–1/6. Thus, the toss of a single die is distributed uniformly.

Figure 2.4 shows the distribution of the sum of the potential results from tossing two fair dice. There is only one way

Figure 2.3 Distribution of the toss of a single die.

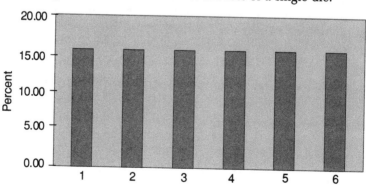

Figure 2.4 Distribution of the toss of two dice.

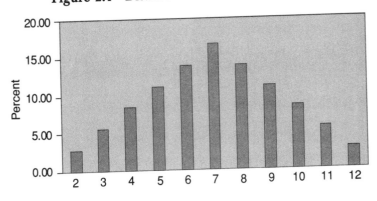

for the outcomes to sum to 2, which is by tossing two 1s. Similarly, there is only one combination that sums to 12. The likelihood of either of these occurrences is 1/36 or 2.78%. There are, however, two possible combinations that sum to 3 and two combinations that sum to 11; hence the likelihood of either of these outcomes is 2/36 or 5.56%. The most likely outcome is 7, for which there is a 16.67% probability. Table 2.1 shows the possible combinations from the toss of two dice and their corresponding probabilities.

When we plot the frequency distribution from Table 2.1, we see that possible outcomes are no longer uniformly distributed. There is a greater probability of experiencing values near the center of the distribution.

As we increase the number of dice (random variables) that we sum to generate our frequency distribution, the more closely it resembles a normal distribution, even though each die by itself produces a uniform distribution.

The normal distribution has convenient properties. The mean (the average value), the median (the middle value),

Table 2.1 Possible combinations from the toss of two dice.

Outcome	Possible Combinations						Probability (%)
2	1-1						2.78
3	1-2	2-1					5.56
4	1-3	3-1	2-2				8.33
5	1-4	4-1	2-3	3-2			11.11
6	1-5	5-1	2-4	4-2	3-3		13.89
7	1-6	6-1	2-5	5-2	3-4	4-3	16.67
8	2-6	6-2	3-5	5-3	4-4		13.89
9	3-6	6-3	4-5	5-4			11.11
10	4-6	6-4	5-5				8.33
11	5-6	6-5					5.56
12	6-6						2.78

and the mode (the most common value) are all the same. The other values under a normal distribution are distributed symmetrically around these equal measures of central tendency. Also, the entire normal distribution is fully specified by its mean and standard deviation. For example, the area under the normal distribution ranging from one standard deviation below the mean to one standard deviation above the mean comprises 68% of all the observations, while the area ranging from two standard deviations below the mean to two standard deviations above the mean comprises 95% of the observations.

Suppose, for example, that an investment's returns are normally distributed with an expected return (mean) equal to 10% and a standard deviation equal to 15%. From the properties of a normal distribution, we know that 68% of the returns lie between −5% (10% − 15%) and 25% (10% + 15%). We also know that 95% of the returns lie between −20% (10% − 2 × 15%) and 40% (10% + 2 × 15%). From this knowledge, we can infer that there is a 16% chance of losing 5% or more because

32% of the returns lie equally outside the one standard deviation range. The highlighted area to the left in Figure 2.5 represents 16% of the area under the normal distribution. Similarly, we can infer that the likelihood of losing 20% or more equals 2.5%.

Before describing how to estimate the likelihood of any particular loss, we must address an important property of investment returns, which I mentioned earlier. Investment returns are not precisely normally distributed, even theoretically. They are what we call lognormally distributed. The fact that investment returns are compounded creates skewness in their distribution. Consider, for example, a positive 10% return compounded over two consecutive periods. Its cumulative two-period return equals 21% $[(1 + 0.10) \times (1 + 0.10) - 1 = 0.21)]$. Now consider a 10% loss compounded over two periods. Its cumulative return equals −19% $[(1 − 0.10) \times (1 − 0.10) − 1 = 0.19)]$. This asymmetry that results from compounding is captured precisely by the lognormal distribution, which is shown in Figure 2.6. Figure 2.6 shows

Figure 2.5   Normal distribution.

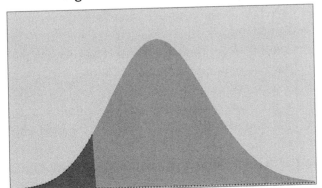

Figure 2.6   Lognormal distribution.

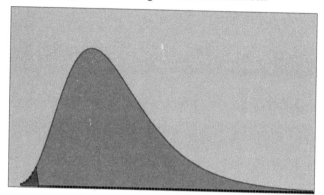

the distribution of five-year cumulative returns to emphasize the effect of compounding. Figure 2.6 reveals that the likelihood of suffering an annualized loss of 5% or more *on average* over five years is much more remote than a 5% loss in any single year, which is explained in the next section.

That periodic returns are lognormally distributed implies that continuous returns are normally distributed, because continuous returns are equal to the natural logarithms of one plus the periodic returns. Therefore, if we wish to use the properties of the normal distribution to estimate an investment's likelihood of loss, we must convert the investment's periodic returns to continuous returns. Then we use the mean and standard deviation of these values, along with the normal distribution, to estimate the likelihood of loss.

We are now ready to estimate the probability of a single period loss. Suppose we wish to estimate the likelihood that an investment in the stock market will produce a loss of 10% or more in a single year and that we are willing to base our estimate on the historical mean and standard deviation from the past 73 years. We begin by converting the periodic annual returns into their continuous counterparts by adding one to the returns and taking the natural logarithms of these values. We then calculate the mean and standard deviation of these continuous returns.

Next we convert our target return of −10% to its continuous equivalent, which equals −10.54% [*ln* (1 − 0.10)]. We then standardize the difference between the continuous target return and the continuous mean by dividing it by the continuous standard deviation. This standardized difference equals −1.0944 [(−0.1054 − 0.1063)/0.1934]. The standardized value, −1.0944, is sometimes called the normal deviate or the standardized variable. It measures how many standard deviation units away from the mean is the target return. Essentially, it re-scales the normal distribution with the actual mean and standard deviation to a normal distribution with a mean of zero and a standard deviation of one.

The properties of the normal distribution enable us to map the normal deviates from this re-scaled distribution onto probabilities. Remember that a normal deviate of minus one standard deviation is 34% below the mean. Thus, there is a 16% (50% − 34%) chance of experiencing a return that is one standard deviation or further below the mean. A return that is 1.0944 standard deviation units below the mean is therefore less likely. The actual probability equals 13.69%.

The conversion of a normal deviate into a probability requires integration, a mathematical procedure that measures the area under a curve—in this case, a normal curve. Fortunately, most statistics books contain normal distribution tables that show the correspondence of normal deviates to probabilities. Moreover, many calculators and spreadsheet software contain functions that perform this conversion. Table 2.2

Table 2.2 Normal distribution table: Positive normal deviates.

	0.00 (%)	0.01 (%)	0.02 (%)	0.03 (%)	0.04 (%)	0.05 (%)	0.06 (%)	0.07 (%)	0.08 (%)	0.09 (%)
3.0	99.87	99.87	99.87	99.88	99.88	99.89	99.89	99.89	99.90	99.90
2.9	99.81	99.82	99.82	99.83	99.84	99.84	99.85	99.85	99.86	99.86
2.8	99.74	99.75	99.76	99.77	99.77	99.78	99.79	99.79	99.80	99.81
2.7	99.65	99.66	99.67	99.68	99.69	99.70	99.71	99.72	99.73	99.74
2.6	99.53	99.55	99.56	99.57	99.59	99.60	99.61	99.62	99.63	99.64
2.5	99.38	99.40	99.41	99.43	99.45	99.46	99.48	99.49	99.51	99.52
2.4	99.18	99.20	99.22	99.25	99.27	99.29	99.31	99.32	99.34	99.36
2.3	98.93	98.96	98.98	99.01	99.04	99.06	99.09	99.11	99.13	99.16
2.2	98.61	98.64	98.68	98.71	98.75	98.78	98.81	98.84	98.87	98.90
2.1	98.21	98.26	98.30	98.34	98.38	98.42	98.46	98.50	98.54	98.57
2.0	97.72	97.78	97.83	97.88	97.93	97.98	98.03	98.08	98.12	98.17
1.9	97.13	97.19	97.26	97.32	97.38	97.44	97.50	97.56	97.61	97.67
1.8	96.41	96.49	96.56	96.64	96.71	96.78	96.86	96.93	96.99	97.06
1.7	95.54	95.64	95.73	95.82	95.91	95.99	96.08	96.16	96.25	96.33

1.6	94.52	94.63	94.74	94.84	94.95	95.05	95.15	95.25	95.35	95.45
1.5	93.32	93.45	93.57	93.70	93.82	93.94	94.06	94.18	94.29	94.41
1.4	91.92	92.07	92.22	92.36	92.51	92.65	92.79	92.92	93.06	93.19
1.3	90.32	90.49	90.66	90.82	90.99	91.15	91.31	91.47	91.62	91.77
1.2	88.49	88.65	88.88	89.07	89.25	89.44	89.62	89.80	89.97	90.15
1.1	86.43	86.65	86.86	87.08	87.29	87.49	87.70	87.90	88.10	88.30
1.0	84.13	84.38	84.61	84.85	85.08	85.31	85.54	85.77	85.99	86.21
0.9	81.59	81.86	82.12	82.38	82.64	82.89	83.15	83.40	83.65	83.89
0.8	78.81	79.10	79.39	79.67	79.95	80.23	80.51	80.78	81.06	81.33
0.7	75.80	76.11	76.42	76.73	77.04	77.34	77.64	77.94	78.23	78.52
0.6	72.57	72.91	73.24	73.57	73.89	74.22	74.54	74.86	75.17	75.49
0.5	69.15	69.50	69.85	70.19	70.54	70.88	71.23	71.57	71.90	72.24
0.4	65.54	65.91	66.28	66.64	67.00	67.36	67.72	68.08	68.44	68.79
0.3	61.79	62.17	62.55	62.93	63.31	63.68	64.06	64.43	64.80	65.17
0.2	57.93	58.32	58.71	59.10	59.48	59.87	60.26	60.64	61.03	61.41
0.1	53.98	54.38	54.78	55.17	55.57	55.96	56.36	56.75	57.14	57.53
0.0	50.00	50.40	50.80	51.20	51.60	51.99	52.39	52.79	53.19	53.59

Table 2.3 Normal distribution table: Negative normal deviates.

	0.00 (%)	−0.01 (%)	−0.02 (%)	−0.03 (%)	−0.04 (%)	−0.05 (%)	−0.06 (%)	−0.07 (%)	−0.08 (%)	−0.09 (%)
0.0	50.00	49.60	49.20	48.80	48.40	48.00	47.60	47.21	46.81	46.41
−0.1	46.01	45.62	45.22	44.82	44.43	44.03	43.64	43.25	42.85	42.46
−0.2	42.07	41.68	41.29	40.90	40.51	40.13	39.74	39.35	38.97	38.59
−0.3	38.21	37.82	37.44	37.07	36.69	36.31	35.94	35.57	35.19	34.82
−0.4	34.45	34.09	33.72	33.36	32.99	32.63	32.27	31.91	31.56	31.20
−0.5	30.85	30.50	30.15	29.80	29.46	29.11	28.77	28.43	28.09	27.76
−0.6	27.42	27.09	26.76	26.43	26.11	25.78	25.46	25.14	24.82	24.51
−0.7	24.19	23.88	23.57	23.27	22.96	22.66	22.36	22.06	21.77	21.47
−0.8	21.18	20.89	20.61	20.32	20.04	19.76	19.49	19.21	18.94	18.67
−0.9	18.40	18.14	17.88	17.62	17.36	17.10	16.85	16.60	16.35	16.11
−1.0	15.86	15.62	15.38	15.15	14.91	14.68	14.45	14.23	14.00	13.78
−1.1	13.56	13.35	13.13	12.92	12.71	12.51	12.30	12.10	11.90	11.70
−1.2	11.51	11.31	11.12	10.93	10.75	10.56	10.38	10.20	10.03	9.85
−1.3	9.68	9.51	9.34	9.17	9.01	8.85	8.69	8.53	8.38	8.22

-1.4	8.07	7.93	7.78	7.63	7.49	7.35	7.21	7.08	6.94	6.81
-1.5	6.68	6.55	6.42	6.30	6.18	6.06	5.94	5.82	5.70	5.59
-1.6	5.48	5.37	5.26	5.15	5.05	4.95	4.84	4.74	4.65	4.55
-1.7	4.46	4.36	4.27	4.18	4.09	4.01	3.92	3.84	3.75	3.67
-1.8	3.59	3.51	3.44	3.36	3.29	3.21	3.14	3.07	3.00	2.94
-1.9	2.87	2.81	2.74	2.68	2.62	2.56	2.50	2.44	2.38	2.33
-2.0	2.27	2.22	2.17	2.12	2.07	2.02	1.97	1.92	1.88	1.83
-2.1	1.79	1.74	1.70	1.66	1.62	1.58	1.54	1.50	1.46	1.43
-2.2	1.39	1.35	1.32	1.29	1.25	1.22	1.19	1.16	1.13	1.10
-2.3	1.07	1.04	1.02	0.99	0.96	0.94	0.91	0.89	0.87	0.84
-2.4	0.82	0.80	0.78	0.75	0.73	0.71	0.69	0.68	0.66	0.64
-2.5	0.62	0.60	0.59	0.57	0.55	0.54	0.52	0.51	0.49	0.48
-2.6	0.47	0.45	0.44	0.43	0.41	0.40	0.39	0.38	0.37	0.36
-2.7	0.35	0.34	0.33	0.32	0.31	0.30	0.29	0.28	0.27	0.26
-2.8	0.26	0.25	0.24	0.23	0.23	0.22	0.21	0.21	0.20	0.19
-2.9	0.19	0.18	0.17	0.17	0.16	0.16	0.15	0.15	0.14	0.14
-3.0	0.13	0.13	0.13	0.12	0.12	0.11	0.11	0.11	0.10	0.10

shows the probabilities associated with a wide, but coarse, range of positive normal deviates, and Table 2.3 on pages 36–37 shows the probabilities associated with negative normal deviates.

Here is how we use a normal distribution table. We look down the left column to −1.0 and across the top row to −0.09. The intersection shows that a normal deviate of −1.09 corresponds to a probability of 13.78%, but we know that this estimate is somewhat coarse because our actual normal deviate is −1.0944. Thus, we look down the left column to −1.1 and across the top row to 0.00. At this intersection the probability equals 13.56%. These two probability estimates bracket the actual probability, which makes sense given that the actual normal deviate falls between −1.09 and −1.10. Thus, we would interpolate to arrive at 13.69%.

MULTIPERIOD ANNUALIZED LOSS

Suppose we have a longer horizon than one year. Instead, we are interested in the performance of our investment over several years. The specific probability we wish to estimate is the likelihood that our investment will depreciate, *on average,* by 10% or more per year over several years. This probability does not imply that our investment will lose 10% or more each and every year. It assumes some annual returns above −10% as long as they are offset by sufficiently low returns to produce an annualized return less than −10%. Let's assume a 10-year horizon to illustrate the point. The relevant normal deviate is calculated by multiplying the annualized continuous returns by the number of years in our horizon and the standard deviation of continuous returns by the square root of the number of years:

$$\frac{(-0.1054 \times 10) - (0.1063 \times 10)}{0.1934 \times \sqrt{10}} = -3.4609$$

This normal deviate corresponds to a probability of 0.03%, which I imagine most investors would consider comfortably remote. If we shorten our horizon to five years the normal deviate increases to −2.4572 and the probability rises to 0.72%, still not a particularly worrisome situation for most investors.

Now let's investigate the likelihood of a cumulative loss over a multiyear horizon.

MULTIPERIOD CUMULATIVE LOSS

The likelihood that our investment will generate a 10% cumulative loss over 10 years corresponds to an annualized loss of 1.05% $[(1 - 0.0105)^{10} = 0.90]$. The only adjustment we need to make to our previous calculation of the normal deviate is to leave the target continuous return as −0.1054 instead of multiplying it by 10. In this case the normal deviate is −1.9104, which corresponds to a 2.80% probability of occurrence. If we again shorten the horizon to five years the probability increases to 7.04%.

In general, if our investment's continuous return is expected to be greater than the continuous target return, a longer time horizon will reduce the probability of a multiperiod loss. Now let's explore the likelihood of experiencing a loss, not on average over our horizon, but in at least one of the years during our horizon.

AT LEAST ONE PERIODIC LOSS

The probability of a loss in one or more of the next 10 years is precisely equal to one minus the probability of not experiencing the loss in every one of the next 10 years. In our earlier example of a single period loss, we estimated the probability of a 10% loss to equal 13.69%. It follows, therefore, that the likelihood of not experiencing a 10% loss in a single year is 86.31% (1.00 − 0.1369), and assuming year to year independence, the likelihood of avoiding a 10% annual loss for 10 consecutive years equals 86.31% raised to the 10th power, which is 22.94%. Thus, there is a 77.06% (1.00 − 0.2294) chance that our investment will lose 10% or more in at least one of the next 10 years. If we shorten our horizon to 5 years, the likelihood falls to 52.10%. In this case, the duration of our investment horizon has the opposite effect on the likelihood of loss. A shorter horizon reduces the number of opportunities for a single period loss.

This standard is much stricter than the earlier standards I described, but it is not unreasonable. A significant single period loss, even if it is likely to be reversed in time, may prompt us to react differently than had we focused only on the final result. It may be overly heroic to assume that we can ignore intermediate outcomes and stay focused on the long run. This line of reasoning leads to another variation on the likelihood of loss—the probability that at some point an investment will fall to 90% of its original value, even if it subsequently recovers.

LIKELIHOOD OF PENETRATING A THRESHOLD

Suppose we are penalized if our portfolio's value ever penetrates a level that is 10% below its initial value. We can apply Equation 2.1 to assess the likelihood of penetrating a threshold. This type of problem is known as a first passage time problem. The probability that an investment will depreciate to a particular value over some horizon during which it is monitored continuously equals:[2]

$$N\left[\frac{ln(C/S) - \mu T}{\sigma\sqrt{T}}\right] + (C/S)^{\frac{2\mu}{\sigma^2}} N\left[\frac{ln(C/S) + \mu T}{\sigma\sqrt{T}}\right] \quad (2.1)$$

where $N[\,] =$ Cumulative normal distribution function
$ln =$ Natural logarithm
$C =$ Critical value
$S =$ Starting value
$\mu =$ Continuous return
$\sigma =$ Continuous standard deviation
$T =$ Number of years in horizon

The symbol $N[\,]$, which is defined as the cumulative normal distribution function, simply refers to the probability that is associated with the normal deviate within the brackets. For example, if the value within the brackets were 1, then $N[\,]$ would equal 84% (Table 2.2).

---

[2] The first passage probability is described in S. Karlin and H. Taylor, *A First Course in Stochastic Processes* (2nd ed.) (New York: Academic Press, 1975).

Again, we assume that the stock market has a 10.63% continuous expected return and a 19.34% continuous standard deviation. By substituting these values into Equation 2.1, we discover that it has a 54.52% chance of falling to 90% or less of its initial value at some point during a 10-year horizon; that is, if we monitor it continuously.

Many economists and policy makers advocate investment of social security funds in the stock market. They support this position by noting the low frequency with which the stock market produces a loss over long horizons. This argument is specious, however, because it assumes implicitly that everyone retires at the end of the same long horizon rather than continually throughout a long horizon. Although the *average* (and, therefore, nonexistent) retiree is unlikely to suffer a significant loss from investment of social security funds in the stock market, it is very likely that many individual retirees will suffer significant losses. This problem is even more acute when we account for variation in the inception of employment across a large population along with variation in retirement dates.

LIKELIHOOD OF PENETRATING A THRESHOLD AT SPECIFIED INTERVALS

Suppose instead that we are only penalized if our portfolio is below 90% of its value at the beginning of the investment horizon on two or more consecutive calendar year-ends. This type of problem is called path-dependent because the probability is conditioned on the path of the strategy. Path-dependent problems are typically difficult to solve by formula. Instead, we employ a numerical method called *Monte*

Carlo simulation to simulate the strategy over and over again and then calculate the frequency of occurrences for the outcome of interest.

The term *Monte Carlo simulation* was introduced by John von Neumann and Stanislaw Ulam when they both worked on the Manhattan Project at the Los Alamos National Laboratory. Ulam invented the procedure of substituting a sequence of random numbers into equations to solve problems relating to the physics of nuclear explosions. The two of them used the term as a code name for the secret work they were conducting.[3] The choice of the name is in honor of one of Ulam's relatives who was known to frequent the gambling casinos at Monte Carlo.

Monte Carlo simulation as it applies to our problem assumes an underlying set of unobservable annual returns that are lognormally distributed. Spreadsheet software have functions that generate random variables from a normal distribution with a mean of zero and a standard deviation of one. We wish to convert the underlying distribution from which the random numbers are drawn to a distribution of continuous returns with a mean of 10.63% and a continuous standard deviation equal to 19.34%. We accomplish this transformation by first multiplying the random numbers from the original distribution by the continuous standard deviation and then adding to these values the continuous mean. We now have a process that generates random continuous returns from a normal distribution with a mean of 10.63% and a standard deviation of 19.34%.

---

[3] M. Browne, "Coin Tossing Computers Found to Show Subtle Bias," *New York Times* (January 12, 1993).

Then we convert these continuous returns into periodic returns and compute the cumulative wealth each year.

Suppose we generate 1,000 random 10-year paths for our investment, and we observe the investment's simulated values along each of these paths at each year-end. To assess the likelihood that our investment will fall to 90% of its initial value on two or more consecutive year-ends we simply calculate the fraction of paths for which this event happens at least once. I performed this simulation and discovered that 138 of the 1,000 paths had at least one sequence in which the 90% threshold was breached on two or more consecutive year-ends. Thus we conclude that the likelihood of this occurrence is 13.8%.

THE BOTTOM LINE

The likelihood of loss depends critically on how we frame the question. I have answered this question six different ways, all for the same investment, the same underlying distribution, and the same loss, and the answers range from 0.03% to 77.06%. These results are summarized:

Likelihood of a 10% Loss

Expected Return = 13.17%

Standard Deviation = 20.26%

1. Likelihood of a single year loss:	13.69%
2. Likelihood of an average annual loss over 10 years:	0.03%
3. Likelihood of a cumulative loss over 10 years:	2.80%

4. Likelihood of a loss in one or more of the next 10 years: 77.06%

5. Likelihood of a cumulative loss at some point over the next 10 years (monitored continuously): 54.52%

6. Likelihood of a cumulative loss on two or more consecutive year-ends over the next 10 years: 13.80%

It pays to know what you are asking.

CHAPTER 3

Time Diversification

Conventional wisdom suggests that investors should be more tolerant of risk if they have long horizons than if they have short horizons, because the likelihood of loss diminishes with time. However, if markets follow a random walk, this view is mathematically false for investors whose behavior accords with the most widely accepted description of risk aversion.

In one of his many landmark articles, Paul A. Samuelson showed that investors should not change their exposure to risky assets based on their time horizon.[1] Samuelson's insight was inspired by a conversation he had with one of his MIT colleagues. Samuelson offered his colleague a risky gamble in which his colleague would be favored to win. His

---

Many of the ideas in this chapter were developed jointly with Don Rich and presented in M. Kritzman and D. Rich, "Beware of Dogma: The Truth about Time Diversification," *The Journal of Portfolio Management* (summer 1998), pp. 66–77.

[1] P.A. Samuelson, "Risk and Uncertainty: A Fallacy of Large Numbers," *Scientia* (April/May 1963), pp. 1–6.

colleague refused this favorable gamble claiming that he could not afford to lose the amount of money that he would place at risk. He countered, however, that he would be willing to engage in a large number of these gambles, each at the same stake as the one he refused. He reasoned that the law of large numbers would ensure his success. Investors use the same logic to support the conventional wisdom that it is safer to invest in risky assets over long horizons than short horizons. The conventional wisdom follows from the observation that over long horizons above average returns tend to offset below average returns. Samuelson's contradiction of this notion is the basis of the time diversification controversy.

To evaluate this controversy, we need to understand precisely what Samuelson demonstrated. He showed that investors should not conclude that it is safer to allocate more of their wealth to risky assets over longer horizons if the following conditions hold and their intent is to maximize expected utility:

1. Investors have constant relative risk aversion, which means that they maintain the same percentage exposure to risky assets regardless of changes in wealth.

2. Investment returns are independent and identically distributed, which means that they follow a random walk.

3. Future wealth depends only on investment results and not on human capital or consumption habits.

If these assumptions hold, it follows mathematically that Samuelson's result is true. Nonetheless, many of his critics seem undeterred by mathematical truth. They reject his

conclusion on the grounds that annualized volatility decreases with time and that the probability of loss also falls
with time. They seem, however, to ignore the fact that the
distribution of terminal wealth increases with time, thereby
raising the potential magnitude of loss.

Consider, for example, an investment that has an annualized continuous return of 10% and an annualized standard deviation of continuous returns equal to 20%. Table 3.1 shows
the annual standard deviation, the cumulative standard deviation, the standard deviation of annualized returns, the probability of loss, and the fraction of wealth that could be lost
given a 1 out of 1,000 probability, all as a function of horizon.

These results reveal that if risk is construed as *annualized
variability*, then time diminishes risk. Portfolio managers
whose contribution is measured by the Sharpe ratio (Excess
Return / Standard Deviation) might fall into this category. If

Table 3.1 What is risk?

	Investment Horizon, T (Years)			
	1	5	10	20
Annual standard deviation, σ (%)	20.00	20.00	20.00	20.00
Cumulative standard deviation, $\sigma\sqrt{T}$ (%)	20.00	44.72	63.25	89.44
Standard deviation of annualized returns, $\sigma/\sqrt{T}$ (%)	20.00	8.94	6.32	4.47
Probability of loss on average over horizon, $N(-0.1/\sigma)$ (%)	30.85	13.18	5.69	1.27
Fraction of wealth lost, 1 out of 1,000 (%)	40.50	58.43	61.48	73.92

risk is perceived as the likelihood of loss, again risk declines with time. Investors who are required to maintain a minimum reserve might view risk in this context. However, if the *magnitude* of potential loss defines risk, then it increases with time. The truth is that risk has no universal definition; rather, like beauty, it is in the eyes of the beholder.

The time diversification debate, for many, has degenerated into a referendum on the meaning of risk, which is futile. For others, it is a debate about mathematical truth, which is absurd. What merits debate are Samuelson's assumptions.

A NUMERICAL DEMONSTRATION OF SAMUELSON'S INSIGHT

The impact of time horizon on one's preference for risky assets is objectively demonstrable. The willingness of an investor to take more risk over a longer horizon than a shorter horizon depends upon the nature of the investor's view of wealth, commonly referred to as the investor's utility function (a utility function is simply a formula that maps varying amounts of wealth onto one's perception of his or her well-being).

The notion of utility was first introduced by the famous mathematician, Daniel Bernoulli. He is one of several celebrated Bernoulli mathematicians. His father, Johann, made significant contributions to calculus, although much of his work was published by the Marquis de l'Hôspital. Johann was also the mentor of the famous prodigy, Leonhard Euler. The most renowned Bernoulli was Daniel's uncle and Johann's older brother, Jakob, who is known mostly for his contributions to the theory of probability. Finally, Daniel's

The Saint Petersburg Paradox

The Saint Petersburg Paradox poses the following question: How much would you be willing to pay to enter a coin tossing game with the following payoff? You win $1 for a head and nothing for a tail. If you win you may toss again. On the second toss you win $2 for a head. Again, if you win you have the opportunity to play again. This time a head yields $4. As long as you continue to toss heads the game continues and the payoff doubles for each head you toss.

The paradox is that the expected value of this game is infinity ($0.50 \times \$1 + 0.25 \times \$2 + 0.125 \times \$4 + \ldots$), but people whose utility is described by a log-wealth utility function would not be willing to pay more than two dollars to play this game. The utility or satisfaction that it conveys increases at a decreasing rate up to a limit of 0.693, and the certainty equivalent of this amount of utility is only two dollars, as shown:

Consecutive Heads	Probability (%)	Payoff	Expected Value	Cumulative Expected Value	Expected Utility	Cumulative Expected Utility	Certainty Equivalent
1	50.0000	1	0.50	0.50	0.0000	0.0000	1.0000
2	25.0000	2	0.50	1.00	0.1733	0.1733	1.1892
3	12.5000	4	0.50	1.50	0.1733	0.3466	1.4142
4	6.2500	8	0.50	2.00	0.1300	0.4765	1.6105
5	3.1250	16	0.50	2.50	0.0866	0.5632	1.7563
6	1.5625	32	0.50	3.00	0.0542	0.6173	1.8540
7	0.7813	64	0.50	3.50	0.0325	0.6498	1.9152
8	0.3906	128	0.50	4.00	0.0190	0.6688	1.9519
9	0.1953	256	0.50	4.50	0.0108	0.6796	1.9731
10	0.0977	512	0.50	5.00	0.0061	0.6857	1.9852
11	0.0488	1,024	0.50	5.50	0.0034	0.6891	1.9919
12	0.0244	2,048	0.50	6.00	0.0019	0.6909	1.9956
13	0.0122	4,096	0.50	6.50	0.0010	0.6920	1.9976
14	0.0061	8,192	0.50	7.00	0.0005	0.6925	1.9987
15	0.0031	16,384	0.50	7.50	0.0003	0.6928	1.9993

cousin, Nicholas Bernoulli, was a distinguished mathematician who proposed the famous Saint Petersburg Paradox, for which Daniel offered a solution in his classic risk measurement paper.

Daniel Bernoulli proposed that the utility of a gain depends on the particular circumstances of the person making the estimate. He observed, for example, ". . . there is no doubt that a gain of one thousand ducats is more significant to a pauper than to a rich man though both gain the same amount."[2]

Bernoulli averred that for the typical investor utility is equal to the logarithm of wealth. A log-wealth utility function is one of a family of utility functions for which each additional increment of wealth is worth less to the investor than the previous increment. In other words, a given increment of wealth means more to a poor person than it will mean to a wealthy person. By the same token, losses or shrinkages in wealth, grow in importance as they mount. Economists assume that most investors have utility functions that roughly resemble this shape, which is depicted in Figure 3.1.

For a given utility function, we can identify a risky investment that conveys the same utility as a certain gain. This relationship is called a certainty equivalent. Consider a risky investment that has a 50% chance of a 1/3 gain and a 50% chance of a 1/4 loss—for example, an investment of $100 that has an equal chance of growing to $133.33 or diminishing to $75.00. An investor with a log-wealth utility function will be indifferent between allocating $100 to this risky investment and leaving the $100 uninvested, because both alternatives yield 4.6052 units of utility.

---

[2] D. Bernoulli, "Exposition of a New Theory on the Measurement of Risk," *Econometrica* (January 1954). Translation from 1738 version.

Figure 3.1 Log-wealth utility function.

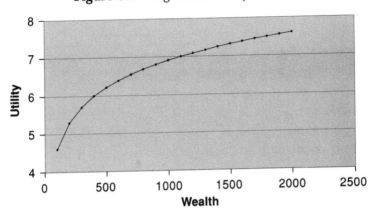

That is, the natural log of $100 is 4.6052, but $[0.5 \times \ln(\$133.33) + 0.5 \times \ln(\$75)]$ also equals 4.6052.

Samuelson's conclusion rests on the fact that risky investments of this type have the same expected utility or attraction for these kinds of investors, regardless of the time horizon involved and even though their expected value increases with time, as Table 3.2 demonstrates.

The moral of this story is that, for investors with log-wealth utility functions, their indifference between a riskless investment and a risky investment of equal expected utility persists irrespective of whether the investment horizon is one year or twenty years or infinity. Moreover, this result is not restricted to investors with log-wealth utility functions. It applies to all investors who have constant relative risk aversion as long as returns follow a random walk. If this were not true, we would observe an increase in expected utility as the number of periods of the investment increases.

Table 3.2   Utility = ln(wealth).

	Initial Wealth	First Period Distribution	Second Period Distribution	Third Period Distribution
				237.04 × .125
			177.78 × .25	
				133.33 × .125
		133.33 × .50		
				133.33 × .125
			100.00 × .25	
				75.00 × .125
	100.00			
				133.33 × .125
			100.00 × .25	
				75.00 × .125
		75.00 × .50		
				75.00 × .125
			56.25 × .25	
				42.19 × .125
Expected wealth	100.00	104.17	108.51	113.03
Expected utility	4.6052	4.6052	4.6052	4.6052

EXPECTED UTILITY WHEN
RETURNS ARE NOT RANDOM

Let's explore the impact of time on expected utility when returns are *not* perfectly random. In the previous example, we
implicitly assumed randomness by specifying an equal chance
of an increase or decrease each period. Instead, let's suppose
that returns follow a mean reverting process, which implies
that an increase is more likely to occur if it is preceded by a
decrease and vice versa. Specifically, we will assume that the
probability of an increase given an immediately prior decrease is 60%, but that the probability of an increase falls to

40% if it follows an increase. It turns out that expected utility is again invariant to time for log-wealth investors, which you can prove to yourself by adjusting the probabilities in the previous table.

The fraction of wealth in the United States allocated to risky assets together with the historical risk premium of U.S. stocks seems to indicate that most investors are more risk averse than log-wealth. These investors will experience an increase in expected utility as their horizon increases under a mean reverting return process. Although they are indifferent between the riskless investment and the risky alternative for a single period, as they continue to invest over multiple periods their indifference shifts to a preference for the risky asset as evidenced by its increasing expected utility. The intuition for this result is that mean reversion causes wealth invested in a risky asset to disperse at a sufficiently slow rate so that conservative investors can tolerate greater exposure to risky assets over longer horizons.

A more conservative utility function is one in which utility equals −1 divided by wealth (Table 3.3). To see that this utility function is more conservative than log-wealth, compare the rate of decline in utility as wealth declines. If wealth declines from $100 to $90, a log-wealth investor will experience a 2.29% drop in utility because 4.4998 (the natural logarithm of 90) is 2.29% less than 4.6052 (the natural logarithm of 100). By contrast, an investor with a utility function equal to −1/wealth will experience an 11.11% decline in utility for the same reduction in wealth because −1/90 is 11.11% lower than −1/100.

The opposite is true for investors who are less risk averse than log-wealth under a mean reverting return process. For

Table 3.3 Utility = −1/wealth.

	Initial Wealth	First Period Distribution	Second Period Distribution	Third Period Distribution
				237.04 × .08
			177.78 × .20	
		133.33 × .50		142.22 × .12
				142.22 × .18
			106.67 × .30	
				85.33 × .12
	100.00			
				142.22 × .12
			106.67 × .30	
		80.00 × .50		85.33 × .18
				85.33 × .12
			64.00 × .20	
				51.20 × .08
Expected wealth	100.00	106.67	112.35	118.63
Expected utility	−0.0100	−0.0100	−0.0099	−0.0098

these investors, the risky investment will generate decreasing expected utility with increases in the number of investment periods. Hence, their indifference between a riskless investment and a risky investment over a single period shifts to a preference for the riskless investment as their horizon increases. The intuition for this result is that mean reversion causes wealth invested in a risky asset to disperse too slowly for investors who are more tolerant of risk.

The impact of nonrandomness on expected utility is summarized as follows: If investment returns are independent and identically distributed, then variance increases proportionally with time, and expected utility is invariant to one's horizon for any utility function that conforms to constant relative risk aversion. Under these conditions investors will prefer to hold constant their exposure to risky assets as their horizon increases.

If, instead, investment returns mean revert, then variance increases at a decreasing rate with time and the following relationships hold:

- Investors who are more risk averse than a log-wealth investor will experience an increase in expected utility as their horizon expands and therefore prefer to increase their exposure to risky assets.

- Investors who are less risk averse than a log-wealth investor will experience a decrease in expected utility as their horizon expands and therefore prefer to reduce their exposure to risky assets.

- Investors who have log-wealth utility will experience no change in expected utility as their horizon expands and therefore will prefer to hold constant their exposure to risky assets.

The opposite is true if investment returns mean *avert,* which means that an increase in the risky asset is more likely than not if it is immediately preceded by an increase and vice versa. A mean averting return process will cause variance to increase at an increasing rate with time. The intuition behind the mean reversion result applies in reverse to explain the preference for risky assets under a mean averting process. These relationships are summarized in Table 3.4.

Table 3.4 The preference for risky assets as a function of time.

Return Process	More Risk Averse Than Log-Wealth	Log-Wealth	Less Risk Averse Than Log-Wealth
Mean reversion	Increase risky assets	Hold constant risky assets	Decrease risky assets
Random	Hold constant risky assets	Hold constant risky assets	Hold constant risky assets
Mean aversion	Decrease risky assets	Hold constant risky assets	Increase risky assets

The historical record appears to support the view that stock returns mean revert.[3] Thus, investors who are more risk averse than log-wealth might be justified to increase risk as their horizons expand. The observation of mean reversion, however, may be illusory owing to biases introduced by survival. For example, if a market has survived it is likely to have mean reverted, whereas if it has disappeared it obviously mean averted because it must have experienced a sequence of losses. Because we don't observe failed markets, the evidence is biased in favor of mean reversion. If we were to include returns from failed markets, the case for mean reversion would most likely appear less compelling.

---

[3] For example, see J. Poterba and L. Summers, "Mean Reversion in Stock Prices: Evidence and Implications," *Journal of Financial Economics* (October 1988), pp. 27–59.

OTHER CONSIDERATIONS
FOR EXPECTED UTILITY

Samuelson's conclusion also relies on the assumption that investors have constant relative risk aversion.[4] It may be the case that some investors have discontinuous utility functions in that utility drops abruptly if wealth penetrates a particular threshold but remains constant or declines at a much slower rate with further reductions in wealth. Such a utility function might be associated with the following situations:

- A decline in the value of pension assets will cause a net pension liability to appear on a company's balance sheet.
- A covenant on a loan agreement will be breached if assets fall below a specified value.
- Your spouse or partner will abandon you if your net worth falls by a certain amount.

Because the probability of incurring a specific loss is lower at the end of a long horizon than a short horizon (assuming a positive expected return) investors with a discontinuous

---

[4] That a typical investor has constant relative risk aversion is a convenient assumption but not necessarily a realistic one. For alternative views on investor utility and their investment implications, see S. Ross, "Adding Risks: Samuelson's Fallacy of Large Numbers Revisited," *Journal of Financial and Quantitative Analysis* (September 1999), pp. 323–339, and K. Fisher and M. Statman, "A Behavioral Framework for Time Diversification," *Financial Analysts Journal* (May/June 1999), pp. 88–97.

utility function will prefer a higher allocation to risky assets over long horizons than they will over short horizons.

The final assumption that underlies Samuelson's result is that future wealth depends only on investment results and not on human capital or consumption habits. The logic is as follows: There are three sources of wealth appreciation: investment returns, wages, and the fraction of wages saved. When we are young we have more human capital to apply toward increasing wages. Moreover, we have greater flexibility to adjust our consumption habits to counterbalance the volatility of terminal wealth that arises from exposure to risky assets.

THE OPTION ANGLE

Some have argued that option pricing theory offers evidence that risky assets grow riskier with time.[5] They assert that because the cost of insurance (a protective put option) increases with time, risk must also increase with time. Otherwise, investors would be unwilling to pay a higher premium for longer dated options. Unfortunately, this line of reasoning has introduced much confusion. This argument does not provide independent verification of Samuelson's result, because there is nothing inherent to option pricing theory independent of the dispersion of wealth that bears on the issue. This fact is apparent from the Black-Scholes option pricing formula, which I cover in some detail in Chapter 6. If you

---

[5] Z. Bodie, "On the Risk of Stocks in the Long Run," *Financial Analysts Journal* (May–June 1995).

review the formula you will note that $(t^* - t)$, the symbol for investment horizon, appears in two ways. It is used to discount the strike price which causes a put option's value to fall with time, and it operates on the dispersion of the risky asset's value in such a way that causes the option's value to increase with time. This latter effect is the same effect that explains Samuelson's result.

Table 3.5 illustrates the redundancy of the option argument with Samuelson's original insight. It reveals, for example, that the value of a five-year put option on an asset with an annual standard deviation of 20% and thus a five-year cumulative standard deviation of 44.72% has the same value as a one-year put option on an asset with an annual standard deviation of 44.72%. The point is that the time adjusted volatility estimate that enters the Black-Scholes formula increases either by holding volatility constant and increasing time or by holding time constant and increasing volatility.

Table 3.5   The cost of insurance as a function of time.

Investment Horizon (Years)	Strike Price ($)	Annual Standard Deviation (%)	Cumulative Standard Deviation (%)	Put Value ($)
1	105.13	20.00	20.00	7.97
5	128.40	20.00	44.72	17.69
10	164.87	20.00	63.25	24.82
20	271.83	20.00	89.44	34.53
1	105.13	20.00	20.00	7.97
1	105.13	44.72	44.72	17.69
1	105.13	63.25	63.25	24.82
1	105.13	89.44	89.44	34.53

These put values assume that the underlying asset's value is 100 and that the continuous riskless return equals 5%.

Aside from this time adjusted volatility effect, which determines the dispersion of the risky asset's value, there is nothing unique about the arbitrage-free framework for valuing options that relates to horizon. The option result is preference free whereas Samuelson's result is preference dependent: *Will an investor prefer more or less exposure to risky assets as the horizon changes?*

SUMMARY

The following mathematical truths prevail as long as returns are independent and identically distributed:

- Annualized volatility diminishes with time.
- The probability of terminal loss for positive expected return assets diminishes with time.
- The magnitude of potential loss increases with time.

It is a matter of taste, however, whether the concurrence of these outcomes represents an increase, a decrease, or no change in risk.

These mathematical truths also prevail if investors have constant relative risk aversion and their wealth depends only on investment performance. As the investment horizon expands:

- Log-wealth investors will prefer to hold constant their allocation to risky assets irrespective of whether returns follow a random walk, mean revert, or mean avert.

- Investors who are more risk averse than log-wealth will prefer to hold constant their allocation to risky assets if returns follow a random walk, increase their allocation to risky assets if returns mean revert, and decrease their allocation to risky assets if returns mean avert.

- Investors who are less risk averse than log-wealth will prefer to hold constant their allocation to risky assets if returns follow a random walk, decrease their allocation to risky assets if returns mean revert, and increase their allocation to risky assets if returns mean avert.

Investors who are extremely averse to penetrating a wealth threshold but relatively indifferent to the extent by which they fall below the threshold will prefer to increase their allocation to risky assets as their horizon expands.

Finally, option values increase with time because the dispersion of the underlying asset's terminal value increases with time, even under a mean reverting process. Mean reversion, however, causes wealth to disperse at a sufficiently slow rate to validate higher allocations to risky assets over long horizons for investors who are more risk averse than log-wealth. The coincidence of these facts confirms that there is nothing peculiar to the valuation of options that is relevant to Samuelson's result.

THE BOTTOM LINE

In 1963, Samuelson revealed a mathematical truth. Since then, many in the academic and investment professions have misinterpreted this mathematical truth as a comment on the meaning of risk, which has provoked an interminable and pointless debate. We should instead, debate the plausibility of Samuelson's assumptions:

- Do returns mean revert?
- Do investors have constant relative risk aversion?
- How important is human capital to the investment decision?

CHAPTER 4

Why the Expected Return Is Not to Be Expected

If you accept history as a guide to the future, at least to the extent that history includes within it the potential investment outcomes of the future, then the following two seemingly paradoxical statements are true:

- The expected future wealth of a sequence of returns drawn randomly from an actual historical sample is greater than the wealth actually produced by those historical returns.

- Even if the past truly is representative of the future, the likelihood that your wealth will grow to a sum at least equal to its expected value is less than 50%; hence the title of this chapter.

You may think that these puzzling assertions have something to do with transaction costs, fees, or taxes, but they do not. I invoke the time-honored assumption that the real world is an uninteresting, special case of my model. How can it be then that the future is expected to be better than the past, but that what is expected is improbable because it occurs less than half the time?

Let's begin with the assumption that we base our future expectations of stock market performance on the annual U.S. stock market returns of the past 20 years. Now admittedly this assumption is optimistic; the past 20 years were an unusually favorable anomaly within the context of the long-term record. For illustrative purposes, however, it doesn't matter which historical sample we select. We could choose a sample of below average returns or perhaps more appropriately the sample of all historical returns. Nonetheless, here's what the past 20 years look like. (Table 4.1.)

It was not a bad time to be invested in stocks. In fact, if you had invested $1,000 in the stock market at the beginning of 1979 and reinvested your income and capital appreciation or losses each year, by the end of 1998 your investment would

Table 4.1 Stock market annual returns.

Year	%	Year	%
1979	18.60	1989	31.81
1980	32.42	1990	−3.91
1981	−4.17	1991	30.49
1982	21.40	1992	7.55
1983	22.41	1993	10.48
1984	6.51	1994	1.06
1985	32.27	1995	37.26
1986	18.17	1996	22.45
1987	5.47	1997	33.84
1988	16.23	1998	28.36

have grown to $26,156 (again, invoking academic privilege by ignoring transaction costs, fees, and taxes).

If you assume that yearly returns for the next 20 years will be drawn randomly (with replacement) from the past 20 years, the expected value of a $1,000 investment 20 years hence is not $26,156. Rather it is $29,485, a $3,329 increment over what actually occurred. However, you are more likely than not to be disappointed if you truly expect to realize this amount. Indeed, the likelihood that you will fall short of the amount you should expect is about 60%. This is the paradox of expected value. The amount you should expect is greater than what actually happened, but it is improbable because it is less than 50% likely to occur.

Keep in mind that this paradox assumes that when you draw randomly from the past 20 years you replenish the sample after each draw. Therefore, you probably won't experience the exact same 20 annual returns arrayed in a different sequence. Instead, you are more likely to draw some of the returns twice or more often and others not at all, and it is theoretically possible, although remote, that you could draw the lowest return 20 consecutive times. (The likelihood of this unlucky sequence is only 1 in 100,000,000,000,000,000,000,000,000–which should not be too worrisome unless you are particularly cautious.)

A BOOTSTRAPPING DEMONSTRATION OF EXPECTED VALUE AND ITS IMPROBABILITY

Bootstrapping is a numerical procedure similar to Monte Carlo simulation (see Chapter 2), but it differs in an important way. Monte Carlo simulation randomly selects returns from an underlying theoretical distribution. It assumes implicitly that the shape of our sample distribution is an approximation of the shape of the true unobservable distribution of all returns, past and yet to occur. By contrast, the bootstrapping procedure assumes that the theoretical distribution is only an approximation of reality. The shape of the true distribution of past and future returns is better approximated by the shape of the sample distribution. The sample, however, is but one pass through history and thus an inadequate measure of all possible passes. Nonetheless, we can use it over and over again to create as many passes through history as we would like, all emanating from the original data and therefore preserving history's statistical attributes.

Here is how we bootstrap to verify these assertions about expected value. We first instruct a computer to select one of the returns from the past 20 years, record it, place it back in the sample, and then select randomly again from the replenished sample until we have a new sequence of 20 annual returns. We then instruct the computer to repeat this selection process 10,000 times so that we end up with 10,000 hypothetical 20-year histories, all based on the yearly returns that actually occurred from 1979 through 1998. Next, we instruct the computer to invest $1,000 in each of these 10,000 paths and to compute 10,000 ending values. The average ending value from these 10,000 paths of returns is the expected value; that is, the value we would achieve on average over many, many repetitions of the investment process. I have performed precisely this experiment. Table 4.2 summarizes the results of this experiment.

You don't have to accept these results. You can perform the same experiment yourself, and I guarantee that you will

Table 4.2 Summary of 10,000 histories bootstrapped from actual returns (1979–1998).

Average ending value of initial $1,000 investment (mean):	$ 29,391
Highest ending value of initial $1,000 investment:	$150,542
Lowest ending value of initial $1,000 investment:	$ 2,529
Ending value for which there is an even probability of exceeding or failing to achieve (median):	$ 26,201
Fraction of ending values below average ending value:	59%

obtain results ordinally equivalent to the results in Table 4.2 and very similar in all other respects.

Aside from confirming my earlier assertions that the expected value exceeds the realized value but that it is less than 50% likely, there is another interesting fact revealed by this bootstrapping exercise. The highest ending value of the 10,000 investment paths exceeds the average ending value by a much greater magnitude ($121,151) than the amount by which the lowest ending value falls short of the average ending value ($26,862). This asymmetry arises from the process of compounding, which is the key to explaining the expected value puzzle.

My predictions about expected value and its likelihood of occurrence were derived theoretically and not from the bootstrapping experiment, which explains the slight difference between my predictions and the results from the bootstrapping experiment. Theoretically, the expected value is derived by compounding the initial investment forward by the *arithmetic average* of the sample returns. If we refer back to Table 4.1 we find that the arithmetic average (the sum of the 20 annual returns divided by 20) equals 18.44%. Therefore, based on this sample the expected future value of an initial $1,000 investment is computed as $\$1,000 \times (1.1844)^{20} = \$29,485$ (more precisely, the arithmetic average equals 18.4350%).

However, the median future value; that is, the value for which there is a 50% chance of exceeding or failing to achieve, is derived by compounding the initial investment forward by the *geometric average* of the yearly returns. The geometric average return from Table 4.1 equals 17.73%; hence the median future value is computed as $\$1,000 \times (1.1773)^{20} = \$26,156$ (more precisely, the geometric average return equals 17.727753%).

The median value is the result that would occur from our bootstrapping experiment if we did not replenish the sample after each random draw.

A BRIEF DIGRESSION ON THE GEOMETRIC AVERAGE RETURN

The geometric average return is computed by adding one to each of the yearly returns (these quantities are called wealth relatives), multiplying these values together, raising the product of this multiplication to an exponent equal to the reciprocal of the number of values that were multiplied together, and then subtracting one. Table 4.3 illustrates this process using the annual stock market returns of the past 20 years.

The geometric average return is sometimes referred to as the constant rate of return or the annualized return. Here is how to interpret it. If instead of generating the returns that actually occurred from 1979 through 1998, the stock market produced the same 17.73% return each year, an initial $1,000 investment would have grown to the same ending value of $26,156. Thus the geometric average return measures what

Table 4.3   The geometric average.

Year	Wealth Relatives	Year	Wealth Relatives
1979	1.1860	1989	1.3181
1980	1.3242	1990	0.9609
1981	0.9583	1991	1.3049
1982	1.2140	1992	1.0755
1983	1.2241	1993	1.1048
1984	1.0651	1994	1.0106
1985	1.3227	1995	1.3726
1986	1.1817	1996	1.2245
1987	1.0547	1997	1.3384
1988	1.1623	1998	1.2836
Product of wealth relatives			26.1563
Geometric average			17.73%

actually happened as well as what should happen with even odds of a better or worse result. However–and this is an important however–it does not measure what we should expect to happen on average over many repetitions.

THE INTUITION OF EXPECTED VALUE AND ITS IMPROBABILITY

At this point you should be convinced that the expected value from a particular sample of returns exceeds the realized value of that sample but that a randomly selected sequence of returns from the sample is more likely to fall short of the expected value than to exceed it. If you are still confused about why these facts are true, however, the following numerical example should clarify matters.

Let's assume that we have an opportunity to invest in an asset with only two possible outcomes per year. It can either return 25% or lose 5% with equal probability. Table 4.4 shows the four potential investment paths that could occur given these assumptions.

After one period there is an even chance that an initial $1,000 investment will grow to $1,250.00 or decrease to $950.00. Therefore, the average or expected value after one period equals $1,100.00 which we can also obtain by multiplying the beginning $1,000 investment by one plus the arithmetic average of the potential returns $[1+(25\% - 5\%)/2 = 1.10\%]$. After two periods there are four equally likely outcomes. The investment can increase 25% in the first period to $1,250.00 and then increase 25% again in the second period to $1,562.50. Or it might first increase 25% and then fall 5% producing an ending value of $1,187.50. Or it might experience the reverse of this sequence by first depreciating 5% to $950.00 and then recovering 25% to end up again at

Table 4.4 A numerical demonstration of expected value and its improbability.

Initial Value	Possible Values After 1 Period	Possible Values After 2 Periods
		$1,562.50 \times .25$
	$1,250.00 \times .50$	
		$1,187.50 \times .25$
1,000.00		
		$1,187.50 \times .25$
	$950.00 \times .50$	
		$902.50 \times .25$
Expected value	1,100.00	1,210.00

$1,187.50. Finally, the investment might depreciate 5% in both years, falling to $902.50 after two years.

The average of these four potential outcomes is $1,210.00, which equals $1,000 compounded forward at the *arithmetic average* return of 10%; that is, $1,000 × 1.10² or equivalently, $1,000 × 1.21. Here is how to think about this result. There are four possible two-year investment paths, which are equally likely to occur. If one were to repeat this investment many, many times, the average, and therefore expected ending value, would equal $1,210.00. However, the actual ending value of $1,000 invested at 25% and reinvested at –5% or invested initially at –5% and then at 25% would equal only $1,187.50. This value is equal to the $1,000 compounded forward at the geometric average of these two returns, 8.97%.

What's going on? In a nutshell, the process of compounding causes the distribution of future investment results to become skewed in such a way that there are fewer values in excess of the average value, but they exceed it by a greater amount, on balance, than the amount by which the more plentiful below-average values fall short of the average value. Note that the upper path produces two consecutive returns that exceed the expected return by 15% yielding an ending value of $1,562.50. These two 15% above-average returns cause the ending value to exceed the expected value by $352.50 ($1,562.50 – $1,210.00). Also note that the lower path produces two consecutive 15% below-average returns, which result in an ending value of $902.50. However, the shortfall of this path relative to the expected value is only $307.50 ($1210.00 – $902.50). This example illustrates how compounding pulls the average or expected value above the value that would actually result from a sequence of returns used to estimate the expected value. By contrast, the distribution of the values after just one period is symmetric around the expected value because the returns have yet to be compounded. This example also shows why a particular ending value is more likely than not to fall short of the expected value. Three of the four paths in this example, which are equally probable, lead to ending values below the expected value.

THE BOTTOM LINE

- If you wish to estimate the expected value of an investment from a sample of historical returns, you should compound the initial investment forward at the sample's arithmetic average return.

- This result represents the outcome you should expect to achieve on average over many repetitions of this investment (random selection with replacement), and it will be higher than the result that the actual returns would have achieved.

- You should recognize, however, that the likelihood of achieving a result at least equal to the expected value is less than 50%; thus you should expect to fall short of the expected value most of the time.

- The expected value is an inflated estimate of any *particular* multiperiod investment outcome because compounding causes positive surprises to more than offset negative surprises of equal magnitude in the computation of the average.

- The median future value is the outcome that you should expect to achieve or exceed half the time.

- The median value is estimated by compounding the initial investment forward at the sample's geometric average return, and it corresponds to the value that the sample's returns would have actually produced.
- The median value is consistent with random selection *without* replacement.

CHAPTER 5

Half Stocks All the Time or All Stocks Half the Time

Are you better off by investing half of your wealth in stocks and half in a riskless asset all of the time, or by investing all of your wealth in stocks half of the time and all of it in a riskless asset the other half of the time?

If you care only about expected wealth, you should be indifferent. However, if you also care about risk or utility, you should have a definite preference.

Before I explain why you should be indifferent or prefer a particular strategy, let's agree on a few assumptions. Later on, I will relax the fourth assumption:

1. We expect stocks to have a higher average return than a riskless asset.

2. It is costless to shift between stocks and a riskless asset.

3. There are no taxes.

4. Stock returns are random; hence we cannot anticipate whether stocks will outperform or underperform a riskless asset in any particular period.

Granted, assumptions 2 and 3 are unrealistic; nonetheless, they allow us to isolate an important issue about dynamic efficiency, which is the point of this puzzle. In fact, let's continue with our suspension of reality by considering a hypothetical stock that can produce only two outcomes in a given period: Either it can increase 25% or decrease 5%. Let's also assume that a riskless asset returns 5% each period without variation. These assumptions allow me to illustrate this puzzle with a simple numerical example. Later on, I will use realistic empirical results and mathematics to confirm the solution.

WHY WE MIGHT PREFER A BALANCED STRATEGY

Table 5.1 shows a possible sequence of stock returns that is consistent with the expected relative frequency for the two returns. It also includes the periodic returns of the riskless asset and of the two strategies of interest; one in which we allocate our wealth equally between the two assets each period (balanced strategy), and the other in which we maintain a 100% exposure to the stock during the first half of the horizon and then a 100% exposure to the riskless asset

Table 5.1 Return and cumulative wealth (switching strategy starts with stock).

Period	Possible Stock Returns (%)	Riskless Asset Return (%)	Strategy Returns (%)		Strategy Wealth (%)	
			Balanced	Switching	Balanced	Switching
1	20.00	5.00	12.50	20.00	1.13	1.20
2	−5.00	5.00	0.00	−5.00	1.13	1.14
3	20.00	5.00	12.50	20.00	1.27	1.37
4	−5.00	5.00	0.00	−5.00	1.27	1.30
5	20.00	5.00	12.50	20.00	1.42	1.56
6	−5.00	5.00	0.00	−5.00	1.42	1.48
7	20.00	5.00	12.50	20.00	1.60	1.78
8	−5.00	5.00	0.00	−5.00	1.60	1.69
9	20.00	5.00	12.50	20.00	1.80	2.03
10	−5.00	5.00	0.00	−5.00	1.80	1.93
11	20.00	5.00	12.50	5.00	2.03	2.02
12	−5.00	5.00	0.00	5.00	2.03	2.12
13	20.00	5.00	12.50	5.00	2.28	2.23
14	−5.00	5.00	0.00	5.00	2.28	2.34
15	20.00	5.00	12.50	5.00	2.57	2.46
16	−5.00	5.00	0.00	5.00	2.57	2.58
17	20.00	5.00	12.50	5.00	2.89	2.71
18	−5.00	5.00	0.00	5.00	2.89	2.84
19	20.00	5.00	12.50	5.00	3.25	2.99
20	−5.00	5.00	0.00	5.00	3.25	3.14

during the second half of the horizon (switching strategy). Finally, it shows the cumulative wealth of the two strategies, assuming an initial $1.00 investment.

The possible stock returns do not occur randomly in this example; they exhibit reversals. Nonetheless, there are an equal number of positive and negative returns, which is what we would expect if we were to select a very large sample of these returns randomly.

The balanced strategy produces the average of the stock return and the riskless return each period. The switching strategy produces the stock returns for the first 10 periods and then the riskless return for the next 10 periods. The two right columns show the growth of $1.00 invested in the respective strategies. The wealth allocated to the switching strategy grows at a faster pace during the first 10 years, because the stock has a higher average return [(20.00% × 0.50) + (–5% × 0.50) = 7.50%] than the balanced strategy [(20.00 × 0.50 + 5.00% × 0.50) × 0.50 + (–5.00% × 0.50 + 5.00% × 0.50) × 0.50 = 6.25%]. In the second 10 years, the balanced strategy out-performs the switching strategy because the switching strategy now produces a 5.00% return each year.

Intuitively, it seems as though both strategies have the same exposure to stocks, on balance, over the full horizon. The balanced strategy is half exposed all of the time whereas the switching strategy is fully exposed half of the time. Intuition, however, is not always the best arbiter of truth. The average per period exposure to stocks of an initial $1.00 allocation to the balanced strategy is $0.9551. By con-trast, the average per period exposure of the switching strat-egy is only $0.8234. This difference accounts for the fact that the balanced strategy produces a higher ending value ($3.25) than the switching strategy ($3.14).

You might suspect that I contrived this numerical exam-ple to generate this difference by starting the switching strat-egy in stocks and then switching to the riskless asset. Table 5.2 shows that the sequence of the switches is irrelevant. The switching strategy, in this example, starts in the riskless asset and then switches to stocks.

The same cumulative wealth is generated by the switch-ing strategy regardless of the sequence of switches. Even if the switches occur every period, the result will be the same as long as the number of periods in which the strategy is exposed to stocks equals the number of periods that it is

Table 5.2 Return and cumulative wealth (switching strategy starts with riskless asset).

Period	Possible Stock Returns (%)	Riskless Asset Return (%)	Strategy Returns (%)		Strategy Wealth (%)	
			Balanced	Switching	Balanced	Switching
1	20.00	5.00	12.50	5.00	1.13	1.05
2	−5.00	5.00	0.00	5.00	1.13	1.10
3	20.00	5.00	12.50	5.00	1.27	1.16
4	−5.00	5.00	0.00	5.00	1.27	1.22
5	20.00	5.00	12.50	5.00	1.42	1.28
6	−5.00	5.00	0.00	5.00	1.42	1.34
7	20.00	5.00	12.50	5.00	1.60	1.41
8	−5.00	5.00	0.00	5.00	1.60	1.48
9	20.00	5.00	12.50	5.00	1.80	1.55
10	−5.00	5.00	0.00	5.00	1.80	1.63
11	20.00	5.00	12.50	20.00	2.03	1.95
12	−5.00	5.00	0.00	−5.00	2.03	1.86
13	20.00	5.00	12.50	20.00	2.28	2.23
14	−5.00	5.00	0.00	−5.00	2.28	2.12
15	20.00	5.00	12.50	20.00	2.57	2.54
16	−5.00	5.00	0.00	−5.00	2.57	2.41
17	20.00	5.00	12.50	20.00	2.89	2.90
18	−5.00	5.00	0.00	−5.00	2.89	2.75
19	20.00	5.00	12.50	20.00	3.25	3.30
20	−5.00	5.00	0.00	−5.00	3.25	3.14

exposed to the riskless asset. These numerical examples seem to suggest that we should prefer the balanced strategy because it generates greater wealth than the switching strategy. Is this conclusion premature?

WHY WE MIGHT BE INDIFFERENT

Consider what would happen if we repeated this experiment many, many times but we flipped a coin to determine whether the switching strategy should be invested in stocks or the riskless asset. The expected return of the switching strategy would equal 6.25%. Interestingly, the expected return of the balanced strategy would also equal 6.25%. We should expect to end up with the same amount of wealth[1] regardless of whether we follow a balanced strategy or a switching strategy, which might lead us to believe that we should be indifferent between the two strategies.[2]

Perhaps you think that these results are an artifact of the simple binary outcome that I imputed to the hypothetical stock. It turns out that if we evaluated these two strategies with actual stock returns, the average return of many repetitions of these strategies would be extremely similar and, in the limit, identical. Table 5.3 shows the annual returns of the U.S. stock market from 1979 through 1998, along with the yearly returns of the balanced strategy and two switching strategies. The first switching strategy starts out in stocks and switches to the riskless asset every other year. The second switching strategy instead starts out in the riskless asset and then switches to stocks every other year.

These results reveal that the balanced strategy produces a lower average return than the switching strategy that begins in stocks, but it exceeds the average return of the switching strategy that starts out in the riskless asset. These results are specific to this particular 20-year history; hence we cannot generalize them. We can, however, create repetitions of this

---

[1] The expected cumulative wealth is 3.36 for both the balanced and switching strategies, which is greater than the cumulative wealth of both strategies reported in Tables 5.1 and 5.2. See Chapter 4 for an explanation of this difference.

[2] See Chapter 4 to understand why the expected ending wealth is equal to initial wealth multiplied by the compounded arithmetic average return and why it exceeds the realized wealth.

Table 5.3 Return and cumulative wealth.

Year	Stock Return (%)	Balanced Return (%)	Switching Stocks First (%)	Switching Riskless First (%)
1979	18.60	11.80	18.60	5.00
1980	32.42	18.71	5.00	32.42
1981	−4.17	0.42	−4.17	5.00
1982	21.40	13.20	5.00	21.40
1983	22.41	13.71	22.41	5.00
1984	6.51	5.76	5.00	6.51
1985	32.27	18.64	32.27	5.00
1986	18.17	11.59	5.00	18.17
1987	5.47	5.24	5.47	5.00
1988	16.23	10.62	5.00	16.23
1989	31.81	18.41	31.81	5.00
1990	−3.91	0.55	5.00	−3.91
1991	30.49	17.75	30.49	5.00
1992	7.55	6.28	5.00	7.55
1993	10.48	7.74	10.48	5.00
1994	1.06	3.03	5.00	1.06
1995	37.26	21.13	37.26	5.00
1996	22.45	13.73	5.00	22.45
1997	33.84	19.42	33.84	5.00
1998	28.36	16.68	5.00	28.36
Average	18.44	11.72	13.42	10.01

20-year sample by bootstrapping it.[3] We draw a return randomly from the sample and place it back into the sample. Then we draw a second return and replace it. We continue in this fashion until we have 20 randomly selected returns. Then we simulate the balanced strategy and the switching strategy. (It does not matter what sequence we choose for the switching strategy as long as the exposure to the stocks and the riskless asset are divided equally.) We then repeat

---

[3] See Chapter 4 for a description of bootstrapping and, in particular, how it differs from Monte Carlo simulation.

this experiment many, many times. I performed this boot-strapping simulation 10,000 times. The average return of the balanced strategy applied to the randomly selected 10,000 20-year histories was 11.76%. The switching strategy generated an 11.75% average return over the 10,000 samples, which supports my assertion that the expected return and thus, the expected ending wealth, are identical in the limit for both strategies.

AGAIN, WHY WE MIGHT PREFER A BALANCED STRATEGY

Should we, therefore, be indifferent between these two strategies? Both are expected to generate the same outcome. Not if we care about risk. It turns out that the switching strategy has significantly greater risk than the balanced strategy. Table 5.4 shows the average return, variance, and standard deviation for both strategies. These estimates are the average values for the 10,000 20-year histories bootstrapped from the actual stock market yearly returns from 1979 through 1998.

Table 5.4 reveals that investors who are risk averse will prefer the balanced strategy to the switching strategy, because for

Table 5.4 Average return and risk.

	Balanced Strategy (%)	Switching Strategy (%)
Average return	11.76	11.75
Variance	0.40	1.20
Standard deviation	6.32	10.95

essentially the same expected return the balanced strategy is significantly less risky than the switching strategy.

I demonstrated the return and risk attributes of these strategies with a conveniently contrived numerical example and with 10,000 random draws from actual historical stock returns. Now let's consider the underlying mathematical process that gives rise to the superiority of the balanced strategy for investors who care about risk. Let the expected return of stocks equal μ_S and the expected return of the riskless asset equal μ_R.

Expected return:

Balanced strategy expected return $= 0.5 \times \mu_S + 0.5 \times \mu_R$

Switching strategy expected return $= 0.5 \times \mu_S + 0.5 \times \mu_R$

The expected return of both strategies is simply the weighted average of the respective expected returns of stocks and the riskless asset. Now let's go through the same exercise for the variance of the two strategies. We will assume that the variance of stocks equals σ^2 and that the riskless asset has no variance.[4]

Variance:

Balanced strategy variance $= 0.5^2 \times \sigma^2$

Switching strategy variance $= 0.5 \times \sigma^2 + 0.5(0.5) \times (\mu_S - \mu_R)^2$

The variance of the balanced strategy's periodic returns is equal to the variance of a portfolio comprising two assets,

---

[4] Even if we substituted a less risky asset with a lower variance than stocks for the riskless asset, we would arrive at the same ordinal result.

To Switch or Not to Switch

One of the more intriguing switching puzzles is based on the long running television game show, "Let's Make a Deal." A contestant would be shown three doors. One of the doors would have a valuable prize behind it, and the other two would not. The contestant would select one of the doors, at which point the host would open one of the other two doors. The host would select a door that he knew not to have the prize behind it. Then the host would ask the contestant if he or she would like to switch to the other door. Is the contestant better off to switch?

Most people believe that there is no advantage to switching. The prize must be behind one of the two remaining doors; hence they assume each door is equally likely to conceal the prize. However, this logic is flawed. The contestant improves his or her odds to two out of three by switching, because the host cannot open the door that conceals the prize or the door selected by the contestant.

Assume the contestant always selects door 1. If the prize is actually behind door 1, the host will open either door 2 or 3. If the contestant doesn't switch he or she wins. If instead the prize is behind door 2, the host must open door 3, and the contestant loses by not switching. Finally, if the prize is behind door 3, the host must open door 2, and again the contestant loses by not switching. The opposite will occur if the contestant switches. Consequently, the contestant has two chances out of three of winning by switching and only one chance out of three of winning by not switching. (See example on page 87.)

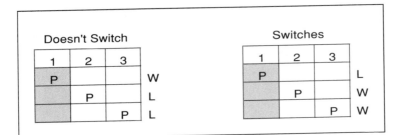

which equals the variance of the first asset times its weighting squared, plus the variance of the second asset times its weighting squared, plus twice the covariance between the two assets.[5] Because the variance of the riskless asset is assumed to equal zero, its covariance with stocks is also zero. Thus the variance of a two-asset portfolio in which one of the assets is riskless is simply the variance of the risky asset times its weighting squared.

The variance of the switching strategy's periodic returns is equal to the variance of stocks times the fraction of the time the portfolio is invested in stocks plus the variance of the riskless asset times the fraction of the time the portfolio is invested in the riskless asset plus a term to account for the fact that the expected returns of stocks and the riskless asset are different.[6] Again, because we assume that the riskless

---

[5] Covariance measures the co-movement of the returns of two assets. Combinations of assets that have low covariances are desirable because they offer greater diversification.

[6] I thank Roger Clarke for alerting me to this adjustment for the difference in expected returns. For a derivation of this formula, see R. Clarke and H. de Silva, "State-Dependent Asset Allocation," *The Journal of Portfolio Management* (winter 1998), p. 63.

asset has no variance, the variance of the switching strategy is equal to the variance of stocks times $\frac{1}{2}$ plus a small term to account for their different expected returns. Hence the switching strategy's variance is expected to equal more than twice the balanced strategy's variance.

IMPLICATIONS FOR MARKET TIMING

Aside from providing an insight with which to torment your friends, this puzzle has important implications for market timing. If you have no market timing skill and you are averse to risk, you should prefer the balanced strategy to the switching strategy. The balanced strategy is dynamically efficient because it offers lower risk for a given level of expected return. It follows, therefore, that to justify a switching strategy you should expect to raise a portfolio's return beyond the expected return of the balanced strategy. In short, you must be skillful at determining in which periods stocks will outperform the riskless asset.

The Sharpe ratio provides a framework for determining how much we should expect to raise return in order to justify market timing. It is defined as a strategy's incremental return over the riskless return divided by its standard deviation. Because it adjusts return for total risk, it is useful for comparing mutually exclusive strategies. Based on our bootstrapping experiment using the prior 20 annual stock market returns and our assumption that the riskless return equals 5%, the balanced strategy's Sharpe ratio equals 1.07 versus 0.62 for the switching strategy. This embedded disadvantage of the switching strategy implies that an investor who engages in such a strategy should expect to add 4.96% as a consequence of timing skill. We arrive at this requirement by solving for the value that will raise the Sharpe ratio of the switching strategy to the Sharpe ratio of the balanced strategy. Here are the relevant inputs:

Balanced strategy average return	11.76%
Balanced strategy standard deviation	6.32%
Switching strategy average return	11.75%
Switching strategy standard deviation	10.95%
Riskless return	5.00%

$$\frac{0.1176 - 0.0500}{0.0632} = \frac{0.1175 - 0.0500 + \alpha}{0.1095}$$

$$\frac{0.0676}{0.0632} = \frac{0.0675 + \alpha}{0.1095}$$

$$1.06962 \times 0.1095 - 0.0675 = \alpha$$

$$\alpha = 0.0496$$

An incremental return of nearly 5% annually would certainly be impressive. This required incremental return, however, assumes that we shift the strategy yearly from one extreme to the other. Alternatively, we may choose to shift within less extreme bounds—say from 25% to 75%—and leave the remainder of the fund equally split between stocks and the riskless asset. This strategy is equivalent to an equal allocation to the balanced and the switching strategy. In this case the required incremental return to justify this limited switching is 1.71%. Note that even though we have reduced by 1/2 the extent to which we engage in the switching strategy, the required increment to expected return to justify switching falls by nearly 2/3. This difference

Table 5.5   Nonlinearity of required skill.

Allocation range	100.00%
Required skill	4.96
Allocation range	50.00
Required skill	1.71
Reduction in allocation range	50.00
Reduction in required skill	65.52

reflects the benefit of diversification that results from blending the balanced and switching strategies. Table 5.5 shows the relationship between required incremental return and the magnitude of the range within which switching is implemented.

SHOULD WE EVER PREFER A SWITCHING STRATEGY?

The Dispositive Answer from Paul A. Samuelson[7]

Thus far, we have focused our analysis on the outcomes at the end of our investment horizon. How much wealth should we expect to accumulate from a balanced strategy versus a switching strategy and how confident should we be of these expected ending results? It may be the case, however, that we care not only about the expected value and dispersion of ending wealth but about interim wealth as well.

---

[7] I thank Paul A. Samuelson for sharing these insights with me after having read a summarized version of this chapter in *Economics and Portfolio Strategy* (June 15, 1999).

After all, we must consume goods and services along the way to survive. Therefore, it is important to determine if a switching strategy might dominate a balanced strategy if we take into account their respective outcomes at different points along our investment horizon.

To answer this question let's calculate the interim expected utility associated with the two strategies and accumulate these values. Utility, in this context, measures the satisfaction or happiness we derive from distributions of wealth associated with the balanced and switching strategies. Let's suppose, for example, that we have a log-wealth utility function.[8] Also, let's suppose that our choices consist of the hypothetical stock that can either return 20% or lose 5% in a given period with equal probability and a riskless asset that returns 6.77% rather than 5% with certainty. We must raise the riskless asset's return from 5% to 6.77%. The reason for these changes is that with a log-wealth utility function, we would not be indifferent between a stock that returns either 20% or −5% with equal odds and a riskless asset that returns 5% with certainty. This stock would always convey greater utility [50% × ln(120) + 50% × ln(95) = 4.6707] than the riskless asset [ln(105) = 4.6540]. This comparison is inappropriate if we have a log-wealth utility function, because we would never allocate 50% of our portfolio to this riskless asset in a balanced strategy or switch to this riskless asset in a switching strategy.

To compare these strategies properly from the perspective of expected utility, we must start with a stock that is the certainty equivalent of the riskless asset. If we raise the riskless asset's return to 6.77%, we would be indifferent

---

[8] See Chapter 3 for a description of a log-wealth utility function.

between the stock and the riskless asset because they both yield 4. 6707 units of expected utility [50% × *ln*(120) + 50% × *ln*(95) = *ln*(106.77) = 4.6707]. These assumptions are summarized as:

Favorable stock return	20.00%
Unfavorable stock return	−5.00%
Riskless return	6.77%
Utility function	Log-wealth

Given these alternatives, a switching strategy generates 9.4069 units of expected utility cumulatively over two periods. In the first period, the switching strategy is invested in the stock. Thus, an initial investment of $100.00 has an equal chance of growing to $120.00 or falling to $95.00, which produces 4.6707 units of expected utility. In the second period, the switching strategy produces 4.7362 additional units of expected utility because the results from the first period grow with certainty at the riskless rate of 6.77%, as shown in Table 5.6.

Table 5.6 Cumulative expected utility of switching strategy.

Initial Investment	First Period		Second Period	
	Wealth Distribution	Utility of Wealth	Wealth Distribution	Utility of Wealth
100.00	120.00	4.7875	128.12	4.8530
	95.00	4.5539	101.43	4.6194
Expected utility per period		4.6707		4.7362
Cumulative expected utility				9.4069

Let's now compute the expected utility of a balanced strategy. There is a 50% chance that an initial investment of $100.00 will grow to $113.39 (50% × 120.00 + 50% × 106.77) which conveys 4.7308 units of utility and a 50% chance that it will grow to only $100.89, yielding 4.6140 units of utility. Thus, the expected utility for the first period equals 4.6724. In the second period, there are four possible outcomes for the balanced strategy, which generate 4.7396 additional units of expected utility. The cumulative expected utility of the balanced strategy over two periods, therefore, is 9.4120, as shown in Table 5.7.

This comparison reveals that the balanced strategy conveys greater expected utility than the switching strategy each and every period and therefore cumulatively. Whether or not we care about interim wealth along with terminal wealth, we should always prefer a balanced strategy to a switching strategy.

Table 5.7 Cumulative expected utility of balanced strategy.

Initial Investment	First Period		Second Period	
	Wealth Distribution	Utility of Wealth	Wealth Distribution	Utility of Wealth
			128.56	4.8564
	113.39	4.7308		
			114.39	4.7396
100.00				
			114.39	4.7396
	100.89	4.6140		
			101.78	4.6228
Expected utility per period		4.6724		4.7396
Cumulative expected utility				9.4120

Indeed, even if we are not indifferent between the stock and the riskless asset, as long as the balanced strategy is optimally split between them, we would still prefer a balanced strategy over a switching strategy, assuming that we have constant relative risk aversion. A mix of a certainty equivalent and a riskless asset is just a special case of an optimal balance, because any blend of a riskless asset and its certainty equivalent is optimal. This preference will always prevail, even if we care about the dispersion of interim wealth.

THE BOTTOM LINE

Assuming we have no market timing skill:

- If we care only about expected return, which is to say we are indifferent to risk, we should be indifferent between a balanced strategy and a switching strategy, because the two strategies have the same expected return.

- If we are risk averse, we should prefer a balanced strategy to a switching strategy, because a balanced strategy has the same expected return as a switching strategy but is less risky.

Assuming we are skillful at market timing and are averse to risk:

- To justify a switching strategy that shifts its exposure between stocks and a riskless asset within a 100% range, we should expect to add almost 5% annually as a consequence of our market timing skill. This result is based on the return and risk of the stock market during the past

20 years and the notion that the switching strategy's Sharpe ratio should be at least as high as the balanced strategy's Sharpe ratio.

- If we reduce the range within which we implement the switching strategy, the incremental return needed to justify switching declines by a greater amount because we benefit from the diversification of blending the balanced and switching strategies.

Assuming we care about interim results along with terminal results:

- If our attitude toward risk is described by constant relative risk aversion, we should always prefer a balanced strategy to a switching strategy because it generates greater cumulative expected utility.

CHAPTER 6

The Irrelevance of Expected Return for Option Valuation

An option grants its owner the right, but not the obligation, to purchase or sell an underlying asset at a pre-established price for a specified period of time. The realized return of the underlying asset determines the option's exact value at expiration. Expectations about this return, however, have no bearing whatsoever on the option's value prior to expiration.

In 1973, Fischer Black and Myron Scholes published an article in the *Journal of Political Economy* entitled "The Pricing of Options and Corporate Liabilities."[1] Thus ended a 75-year search for one of the most elusive solutions to a financial problem. Along the way, some of the most celebrated economists, mathematicians, and scientists contributed (some

---

[1] F. Black and M. Scholes, "The Pricing of Options and Corporate Liabilities," *The Journal of Political Economy,* vol. 81 (1973), pp. 637–654.

Options

The Black-Scholes formula gives the current value of a European call option on a stock that pays no dividends. A European option can only be exercised at expiration. Options that can be exercised prior to expiration are called American options.

Consider, for example, a stock that currently sells for $50 and a call option on this stock with an exercise price (sometimes called a strike or striking price) equal to $55 that expires in three months.

Because a call option does not obligate its owner to purchase the underlying stock, its value at expiration will equal either the stock price less the exercise price if this value is positive, or zero if this value is negative, as shown:

Stock Price at Expiration	Stock Price – Exercise Price	Call Option Value at Expiration
45	−10	0
50	−5	0
55	0	0
60	5	5
65	10	10

A put option grants its owner the right but not the obligation to sell the underlying stock; thus it will be valuable at expiration only if the exercise price exceeds the stock price. Again, if we assume a $55 exercise price, the table on page 99 shows the value of a put option at expiration:

Options

Stock Price at Expiration	Stock Price – Exercise Price	Call Option Value at Expiration
45	−10	10
50	−5	5
55	0	0
60	5	0
65	10	0

Option contracts today are written on a variety of underlying instruments and may include many complicated specifications and contingencies. Although the Black-Scholes formula was derived to value the most basic option contract, valuation models for more exotic option contracts rely on the same underlying principles discovered by Black and Scholes.

unwittingly) to the ultimate solution, including Robert Brown, Louis Bachelier, Albert Einstein, Norbert Weiner, Franco Modigliani, Merton Miller, Paul A. Samuelson, and Robert Merton. The discovery of the Black-Scholes formula was not merely an intellectual victory over a stubborn problem. It elevated our understanding of economics by creating an analytical framework for valuing contingent claims, and it revolutionized the practice of risk management and financial engineering.

Although the media typically portray options transactions as a means for intemperate speculation, in fact, the overwhelming preponderance of options transactions contributes substantially to the amenity of society. They afford producers and service providers a mechanism for hedging their risks, which allows them to offer their products at lower prices than they would otherwise require. This invaluable benefit to society was not lost on the Nobel Prize selection committee. In October 1997, the committee awarded the Nobel Prize in economics to Robert Merton and Myron Scholes for their work in option valuation. Sadly, Fischer Black passed away in the previous year. Although the Nobel Prize is not bestowed posthumously, the selection committee departed from tradition by explicitly citing Black's contribution to the solution of the option pricing puzzle.

THE FORMULA

The celebrated Black-Scholes formula is shown next. Bowing to history, I use the same notation that Black and Scholes used in their article:

$$w(x,t) = xN(d_1) - ce^{r(t-t^*)}N(d_2)$$
$$d_1 = \frac{\ln x/c + (r + 1/2v^2)(t^* - t)}{v\sqrt{t^* - t}}$$
$$d_2 = \frac{\ln x/c + (r - 1/2v^2)(t^* - t)}{v\sqrt{t^* - t}}$$

where $w(x,t)$ = Value of a call option on stock x at time t
x = Stock price
c = Exercise price
r = Interest rate (continuously compounded)
t^* = Maturity date
t = Current date
v^2 = Variance of stock return

ln = Natural logarithm
$N(d)$ = Cumulative normal density function

The Black-Scholes formula may not appear particularly revealing to the uninitiated. Nonetheless, I present it because, without question, it is one of the most significant achievements in the history of economics. Later in this chapter, I will provide an intuitive explanation of the Black-Scholes formula, and I will present an alternative option valuation approach that is considerably more accessible. In the meantime, I would like to draw your attention to the critical innovation of the Black-Scholes formula. It includes no assumptions or expectations about the return of the underlying asset. The expected return of the underlying asset is irrelevant to the value of the option—a detail that was lost on those who preceded Black and Scholes in the quest to solve the option valuation problem. The formula reveals that only five factors determine the value of an option:

1. Price of the underlying asset

2. Exercise price

3. Interest rate

4. Time remaining to expiration

5. Volatility of the underlying asset's return[2]

---

[2] The Black-Scholes formula relies on several simplifying assumptions: (1) the term structure of interest rates up to the option's maturity date is known and constant; (2) the distribution of the underlying terminal stock price is lognormal; (3) the volatility of stock returns is constant; (4) the stock does not pay dividends; (5) there are no transaction costs; (6) it is possible to borrow or lend any fraction of the price of a security at the short-term interest rate; and (7) there are no restrictions on short selling.

THE FOUNDATION

Although options have existed for centuries and achieved widespread usage during the Dutch tulip bulb mania of the seventeenth century, the scientific building blocks of the Black-Scholes formula were discovered much later, and the first rigorous attempt at valuation did not occur until early in the twentieth century. Prior to the discovery of the Black-Scholes formula, investors and speculators relied on heuristic methods to determine at what prices they were willing to purchase or sell options.

The scientific building blocks of the Black-Scholes formula are surprisingly disparate in origin. They emanate from botany, thermodynamics, and corporate finance. A Scottish botanist named Robert Brown made the first important discovery along the option valuation path, although his research was not motivated by an interest in options. In 1827,[3] using a microscope, Brown observed the dispersion of particles within pollen grains suspended in water after water molecules struck them. He noticed that the average position of the particles did not change after they were disturbed, but their dispersion increased proportionally with the amount of time that had elapsed since the initial collision. Today, in honor of Brown, this pattern of dispersion is called Brownian motion. It refers to a diffusion process that is normally distributed with an average change equal to zero and a variance that increases proportionally with the passage of time. Brownian motion describes the behavior of

---

[3] Although he observed this phenomenon in 1827, it was not until the subsequent year that he published the results of his experiments.

a variety of natural phenomena, including, for example, the diffusion of pollutants through the atmosphere.

It was not until 75 years later that a French student named Louis Bachelier invoked the properties of Brownian motion to describe the random behavior of stock prices. Bachelier was a student of the famous probabilist, Henri Poincaré. In 1900, Bachelier successfully defended his doctoral dissertation, *Théorie de la spéculation,* in which he described the mathematical properties of stock prices on Paris' stock exchange, La Bourse.[4] Bachelier assumed that stock prices behaved according to arithmetic Brownian motion. Based on this assumption and by invoking the central limit theorem (see Chapter 2), Bachelier concluded that stock price changes are normally distributed. Bachelier's analysis, however, was slightly flawed because he ignored the effect of compounding on the distribution of stock returns. The process of compounding causes stock returns to conform to geometric Brownian motion, which gives a lognormal distribution of returns instead of a normal distribution.

Bachelier proceeded to derive an option pricing formula that equates the option price to the expected difference between the stock price and the exercise price. Unfortunately, Bachelier's assumption of arithmetic Brownian motion permits negative stock prices as well as option values in excess of the price of the underlying asset, neither of which is possible. Nonetheless, we should not underestimate Bachelier's contribution to modern finance. He initiated the quest for a

---

[4] L. Bachelier, *Théorie de la Spéculation* (Paris: Gauthier-Villars, 1900). Translated by A.J. Boness, in *The Random Character of Stock Market Prices,* P. Cootner, ed. (Cambridge: MIT Press).

rigorous option valuation formula, and his application of Brownian motion, although slightly flawed,[5] was a critical contribution to our understanding of the random nature of asset price fluctuations.

Despite Bachelier's landmark contribution to financial analysis, he labored in relative obscurity throughout his academic career. Owing to the novelty of his work, Bachelier's dissertation committee failed to grasp its significance and refused to award his dissertation "mention trés honorable," a distinction that was a prerequisite for a top tier academic position.

The next person to contribute to the scientific foundation of option valuation was none other than Albert Einstein. In 1905, Einstein provided a rigorous mathematical description of Brownian motion based on the laws of kinetic theory.[6] He derived a formula for the probability that a particle would migrate a certain distance in any direction during a certain time interval given a particular coefficient of diffusion. His formula results in a normal distribution for the displacement of a particle whose variance is a function of the time interval. Einstein's investigation of the mathematical properties of Brownian motion led him to develop an equation for the transfer of heat. As we will see later, this heat exchange equation was critical to the Black-Scholes solution.

---

[5] Bachelier's option valuation formula also assumes that the mean of stock price changes is zero, which unrealistically implies that investors are indifferent to risk.

[6] A. Einstein, "Ueber Die von der Molekularkinetischen Theorie der Wärme Bewegungen von in Ruhenden Flüssigkeiten Suspendierten Teilchen," *Annalen der Physik,* vol. 17 (1905), pp. 549–560.

Einstein's work on Brownian motion was cited, along with his work on the theory of relativity and quantum theory, as the contributions that earned Einstein the Nobel Prize in physics.

The famous MIT mathematician, Norbert Weiner, provided a rigorous mathematical foundation of Brownian motion in his 1918 dissertation.[7] Prior to Weiner's work, the laws of Brownian motion were based on physical properties. He established a purely mathematical model based on the following four assumptions:

1. There exists a normally distributed random variable for any time interval greater than zero.
2. Prior to the passage of time, the value of this random variable is zero.
3. At all future times the expected value of this random variable is also zero.
4. The change in the value of the random variable is independent from interval to interval.

Weiner's model, which is an idealized version of Brownian motion, is referred to as a Weiner process in his honor. His first and fourth assumptions imply that its properties are fully described by the variance of the random variable.

---

[7] Weiner is famous not only for his prodigious mathematical achievements, but for his eccentricity as well. Paul A. Samuelson attributes the following comment to Weiner: "When we met was I walking to the faculty club or away from it? For in the latter case I've already had my lunch." S. Nasar, *A Beautiful Mind* (New York: Simon & Schuster, 1999), p. 136.

In certain applications, including option valuation, it is necessary to relax assumption three and assume that the value of the random variable drifts up or down over time. This variant has come to be known as the generalized Weiner model. Determining the value of this drift was the key innovation of the Black-Scholes formula.

The next breakthrough on the path toward the option solution came from two controversial papers that dealt with corporate finance. In 1958, Franco Modigliani and Merton Miller, economists at Carnegie Tech in Pittsburgh (which today is called Carnegie Mellon University) published an article in the *American Economic Review* entitled "The Cost of Capital, Corporation Finance, and the Theory of Investment."[8] This paper challenged the conventional wisdom that a firm's value depends on its capital structure; that is, its debt/equity mix. Modigliani and Miller invoked the notion of arbitrage to challenge the traditional view of capital structure. They argued that if a leveraged firm is undervalued, investors could purchase its debt and its shares. The interest paid by the firm is offset by the interest received by the investors; thus the investors end up holding a pure equity stream. By contrast, if an unleveraged firm is undervalued, investors can borrow funds to purchase its shares. The substitutability of individual debt for corporate debt guarantees that firms in the same risk class will be valued the same, regardless of their respective capital structures. In essence, Modigliani and Miller argued in favor of the law of one

---

[8] F. Modigliani and M. Miller, "The Cost of Capital, Corporation Finance, and the Theory of Investment," *American Economic Review* (June 1958).

price.[9] This paper generated a huge amount of controversy and resistance, because it effectively rendered irrelevant most of the corporate finance curriculum of the day.

Modigliani and Miller, nonetheless, were not deterred by controversy. In 1961, they co-authored a second paper, "Dividend Policy, Growth, and the Valuation of Shares,"[10] in which they proposed that a firm's value is invariant, not only to its capital structure, but also to its dividend policy. Collectively, these notions are referred to as the MM invariance propositions.

In their second paper, they again invoked the notion of substitutability, arguing that repurchasing shares has the same effect as paying dividends; thus issuing shares and paying dividends is a wash. Although the cash component of an investor's return may differ with dividend policy, the investor's total return, including price change, should not change with dividend policy.

You may wonder what debt/equity ratios and dividend policy have to do with option valuation. Aside from the specific corporate finance issues raised in these papers, MM, as these two papers are generally called, demonstrated the powerful results that could be derived with well-functioning capital markets set against a background of partial equilibrium. Specifically, they used arguments based on arbitrage to demonstrate the irrelevance of capital structure and dividend policy to a firm's value. This proof literally transformed the collective mindset of financial economists, and

---

[9] The law of one price is a time-honored tenet of economics, which hold that assets with the same cash flows must sell for the same price.

[10] M. Miller and F. Modigliani, "Dividend Policy, Growth, and the Valuation of Shares," *Journal of Business* (October 1961).

by so doing, facilitated the later discovery by Black and Scholes that arbitrage renders expected return irrelevant to the value of an option. It is no coincidence that Merton Miller's intervention was required in order for the *Journal of Political Economy* to accept Black and Scholes' article for publication. The *Journal* had previously rejected their submission, but Miller, recognizing its importance, persuaded the editor to reconsider.

I once had an occasion to ask Franco Modigliani if he realized at the time when he and Miller developed their invariance propositions, how influential their work would ultimately be. Without hesitation he replied, "Oh yes, I realized its importance right away by how much it disturbed my colleagues and by how much they resisted our conclusions." It is often the case that important discoveries provoke a confederacy of resistance from those who embrace the established doctrine.

WITHIN EPSILON OF THE SOLUTION

By now the intellectual raw material required by the Black-Scholes formula had been developed, and there were several assaults on the problem before the Black-Scholes success. Recall that in 1900 Bachelier derived an option pricing formula in his dissertation, but he neglected to account for the effect of compounding and the average positive return of stocks. In a 1961 paper entitled, "Warrant Prices as Indications of Expectations,"[11] Case Sprenkle addressed both of

---

[11] C.M. Sprenkle, "Warrant Prices as Indications of Expectations," in *The Random Character of Stock Market Prices*, P. Cootner, ed. (Cambridge, MA: MIT Press, 1964).

these deficiencies. He assumed a lognormal distribution for stock returns, and he included a term for the growth rate of the stock price.

Two additional enhancements to Sprenkle's formula soon followed. James Boness recognized the importance of the time value of money.[12] He used the stock's expected return to discount its terminal value back to its present value. Paul A. Samuelson went a step further and allowed the expected return of the option to vary from the expected return of the underlying stock. In his 1997 keynote address at Mathematical Finance Day, a conference sponsored by Boston University, Samuelson referred to his option formula as "within epsilon of the solution." Epsilon is a Greek letter often used to refer to a vanishingly small quantity.

In fact, the general appearance of the Black-Scholes formula was derived previously in three different papers by Samuelson,[13] Samuelson and Merton,[14] and McKean.[15] These three papers, however, all assumed that the value of an option depends on investor preferences regarding risk, which as we will now see was their critical oversight.

---

[12] A.J. Boness, "Elements of a Theory of Stock Option Value," *Journal of Political Economy*, 72 (1964), pp. 163–175.

[13] P.A. Samuelson, "Rational Theory of Warrant Pricing," *Industrial Management Review* (1965).

[14] P.A. Samuelson and R.C. Merton, "A Complete Model of Warrant Pricing That Maximizes Utility," *Industrial Management Review* (1969).

[15] H.P. McKean, "Appendix: A Free Boundary Problem for the Heat Equation Arising from a Problem in Mathematical Economics," *Industrial Management Review* (1965).

THE BLACK-SCHOLES INSIGHT[16]

In 1965, Fischer Black joined a consulting company near Boston called Arthur D. Little where he met Jack Treynor. At the time, Treynor had been working on a model to price risky assets, which evolved into the celebrated Capital Asset Pricing Model (CAPM). William Sharpe, John Lintner, and Jan Mossin also independently derived the CAPM around the same time, and in 1990, Sharpe was awarded the Nobel Prize for his derivation and economic interpretation of CAPM. Treynor's work received less attention because he chose not to publish it in an academic journal. In any event, Treynor introduced Black, whose formal training was in mathematics and physics, to finance and in particular to the notion of market equilibrium for risky assets. Black and Scholes acknowledged Treynor's role in their quest to derive an option valuation formula with the following note on the first page of their famous article.[17]

In 1969, Myron Scholes had embarked upon an academic career at MIT's Sloan School in Cambridge, Massachusetts, when he met Fischer Black. He and Black soon began to collaborate on the option valuation problem. Proceeding from the earlier work of Sprenkle, Boness, and Samuelson, Black and Scholes soon discovered the key insight that had eluded their predecessors. They recognized that both the expected

---

[16] For an excellent and entertaining history of the Black-Scholes formula and capital market theory in general, see P.L. Bernstein, *Capital Ideas: The Improbable Origins of Modern Wall Street* (New York: Free Press, 1992).

[17] The inspiration for this work was provided by Jack L. Treynor (1961a, 1961b). The references to 1961a and 1961b are to Treynor's unpublished manuscripts on CAPM.

terminal value of a stock and the expected terminal value of an option on that stock are related to the stock's expected return. The option's expected return is related to the stock's expected return through its relative volatility with respect to the stock. Black and Scholes also realized that one could create a hedged position by purchasing a stock and selling call options in a particular ratio, which would cause the impact of the stock's expected return on its price to offset exactly its impact on the option's price.

The ability to create a hedged position implies that options are redundant securities, given a complete stock and bond market. Just as Modigliani and Miller showed that investors can substitute individual debt for corporate debt, Black and Scholes showed that investors could replicate an option by trading the appropriate combination of stocks and the riskless asset.

A hedged position refers to a combination of assets with offsetting returns under all possible states of the world. Because the returns are offsetting, a hedged position has no risk and should therefore yield the riskless return.

Consider, for example, a $100.00 stock today that could either increase 30% or decline 10% over the course of one year. If one were to purchase one share of the stock and at the same time sell short 1 and ⅓ options with a strike price of $100.00, this combination would always produce an ending value of $90.00. If the stock rises to $130.00, the option is worth $30.00 (130.00 − 100.00). A short position of 1 and ⅓ options, therefore, will generate a loss of $40.00 (30.00 × −1.3333) for an ending value on the combined position equal to $90.00. If, instead, the stock falls to $90.00, the option will expire worthless, and the ending value of the combined position will again equal $90.00.

Because the ending value of the hedged position is known today and is riskless, its present value equals its ending value discounted by the riskless rate of return. Suppose the riskless return is 4.00%. Under this assumption, the present value of the hedged position one year ahead equals $86.5385 (90.00/1.04). We now have sufficient information to calculate the present value of the option by setting the components of the hedged position equal to $86.5385 and solving for the option's present value:

$$100.00 - (1 + 1/3) \times \text{Option value} = 86.5385$$
$$\text{Option value} = \frac{100.00 - 86.5385}{(1 + 1/3)}$$
$$\text{Option value} = 10.0962$$

Notice that this calculation of the option's value does not require any input for the stock's expected return. Again, the irrelevance of expected return arises from the fact that with a hedged position the expectation about the stock's uncertain return cancels out.

This example illustrates the key innovation of the Black-Scholes formula; that the riskless return and not the stock's expected return determines the value of an option. You may argue that this example is unrealistic because it deals with a very unusual stock, one that has only two possible outcomes. However, Black and Scholes, with help from Robert Merton, discovered that when we relax this assumption and allow the stock to take on many values through time, the same fundamental principle about the riskless nature of a hedged position applies. In their article, they write:

As the variables x and t change, the number of options to be sold short to create a hedged position with one share of stock changes. If the hedge is maintained continuously, then the approximations mentioned above become exact, and the return on the hedged position is completely independent of the change in the value of the stock. In fact, the return on the hedged position becomes certain.[3]

Note: The variable x refers to the stock's price and t refers to time. Footnote 3 in their article reads, "This was pointed out to us by Robert Merton."[18]

Black and Scholes used this insight of a replicating portfolio to derive the value of an option under the assumption that stock prices change continuously through time. First, they set up a partial differential equation without any terms that depend on investor risk preferences. It simultaneously incorporates two relationships. It relates the change in the value of an option to the change in the value of the underlying stock and the passage of time, and it relates the change in the value of a hedged portfolio and the passage of time to the riskless return. The solution to this equation gives the value of an option.

Neither Black nor Scholes, at first, knew how to derive the solution to these complicated equations, because it required a change of variables to transform this partial differential equation problem into a more tractable ordinary differential equation problem. Once Black and Scholes resolved this problem, they quickly realized that their ordinary differential equation was the same equation as Einstein's heat ex-

---

[18] Black, "The Pricing. . . . "

Differential Equations

A differential equation is an equation that contains one or more derivative terms. Derivatives measure how much a particular variable changes given a vanishingly small change in another variable. An ordinary differential equation contains the derivatives of a single variable, whereas a partial differential equation contains the derivatives of two or more variables.

The value of a call option on a non-dividend paying stock is a function of five variables: the stock price, the exercise price, the riskless interest rate, the volatility of the underlying stock, and the time to maturity. Three of these variables are constant. Still the stock price and time vary. Therefore, the function that relates the option price to changes in the stock price and time is a partial differential equation.

Generally, partial differential equations are difficult to solve analytically unless they can be transformed into ordinary differential equations. This transformation is accomplished by a change of variables, which is how Black and Scholes found their option formula.

---

change equation. It is used to measure heat migration through a substance, and it has a well-known solution that was originally derived by Einstein in his 1905 work on Brownian motion. Black and Scholes used Einstein's solution to the heat exchange equation to derive their famous formula for the value of an option.

A SIMPLE NUMERICAL DEMONSTRATION OF THE IRRELEVANCE OF EXPECTED RETURN

The Black-Scholes formula is an elegant solution to option valuation, but its elegance comes at the expense of flexibility and transparency. Their work, however, provided the insight for the development of alternative valuation methodologies, one of which is called risk neutral valuation. Risk neutral valuation, which was developed by John Cox and Stephen Ross,[19] has the dual virtues that it can be applied to practically any option valuation problem and it is marvelously intuitive.

Let us again return to our simple stock that has only two possible outcomes, a 30% increase or a 10% decrease. Let us also assume that the riskless return is again 4.00%. The present value of an option on this stock with an exercise price of $100 must equal the discounted expected value of the option at expiration. Risk neutral valuation holds that we can use the riskless return to discount the option's expected ending value back to its present value. If we accept this premise of risk neutral valuation, then the probabilities that we assign to a 30% increase and to a 10% decrease are 35% and 65% respectively, because 4.00% equals 0.35 times 30% plus 0.65 times −10%. These probabilities, however, are contrivances that result from risk neutral valuation. They do not truly reflect our views about the relative likelihood of a 30%

---

[19] J. Cox and S. Ross, "The Valuation of Options for Alternative Stochastic Processes." *Journal of Financial Economics,* vol. 3 (1976), pp. 145–166.

increase versus a 10% decrease, nor does risk neutral valuation imply that we are really indifferent to risk.

In any event, if we assume that the stock has a 35% chance of returning 30% and a 65% chance of losing 10%, then a call option on this stock has a 35% chance of returning $30.00 (maximum of 130–100 or 0) and a 65% chance of returning nothing (maximum of 90–100 or 0). We, therefore, calculate the present value of this option by discounting 35% of $30 or $10.50 by 1.04, which equals $10.0962. Let me repeat this logic:

1. The stock will either increase 30% or decrease 10%.

2. Risk neutral valuation posits that we discount the option's expected terminal value by the riskless return, which we assume equals 4.00%.

3. A 4.00% discount rate is consistent with a 35% chance of a 30% increase and a 65% chance of a 10% decrease.

4. The option at expiration will be worth $30 if the stock rises 30% and nothing if the stock declines 10%.

5. It's present value, therefore, equals $(0.35 \times \$30 + 0.65 \times \$0)/1.04$, which is $10.0962.

Risk neutral valuation allows us to discount an option's expected ending value by the riskless return in order to derive its present value. It does not imply—and this is critical—that we actually believe the option's expected return equals the riskless return. We believe that its expected return is related to the stock's expected return through its relative volatility with the stock. I will now demonstrate that by using the option's true expected return to discount its ending value to its present value, we arrive at the same price as we do by using the riskless return. Consider, for a minute, the significance of this equivalence. We do not need to know the stock's expected return in order to value an option on this stock. Whether we overestimate it or underestimate it is irrelevant, because our errors will always cancel out; thus we only need to know the riskless return which is readily observable. In effect, this result represents another invariance proposition: if we can create a hedged position, the value of an option is invariant to the expected return of the underlying asset.

Suppose that we truly believe the stock has an equal chance of increasing 30% or falling 10%. Under this assumption its expected return equals 10%, not 4% (0.50 × 30% + 0.50 × −10%). What does a 10% expected return for the stock imply for the option's expected return? Earlier I mentioned that an option's expected return is related to the stock's expected return through its relative volatility with the stock. Specifically, an option's expected return is equal to its beta with respect to the stock times the stock's expected return in excess of the riskless return.

Beta is a product of the Capital Asset Pricing Model (CAPM) and measures an asset's risk relative to another asset. In 1952, Harry Markowitz showed how to combine assets to form efficient combinations; that is, portfolios, which for a given level of risk offer the highest expected return.[20] He demonstrated that the volatility of a combination of assets depends importantly on the co-movement between the assets. Combinations of assets that tend not to

---

[20] H. Markowitz, "Portfolio Selection," *Journal of Finance* (March 1952).

The Prodigy

The number of risk parameters in a portfolio equals the sum of the number of assets it includes. For example, 5,050, the total number of volatilities and correlations for a 100 asset portfolio equals $1 + 2 + 3 + \ldots + 100$.

There is an amusing and perhaps apocryphal story about this result and the famous mathematician Carl Friedrich Gauss, who was born in 1777 in Braunschweig, Germany. When Gauss was a child at St. Catherine elementary school, his teacher who was named Büttner asked the students in his class to sum the numbers from one to 100. Büttner's intent was to distract the students for a while so that he could tend to other business. To Büttner's surprise and annoyance, however, Gauss, after a few seconds, raised his hand and gave the answer–5,050. Büttner was obviously shocked at how quickly Gaus could add, but Gauss confessed that he had found a short cut. He described how he had begun by adding one plus two plus three but became bored and starting adding backward from 100. He then noticed that one plus 100 equals 101, as does two plus 99 and three plus 98. He immediately realized that if he multiplied 100 by 101 and divided by two, so as not to double count, he would arrive at the answer.

Young Gauss' formula gives the number of risk parameters for a portfolio comprising any number of assets–n times $(n + 1)$ divided by 2, where n represents the number of assets in the portfolio.

move together offer more diversification than assets that tend to move in tandem. Markowitz showed that it is possible to identify the specific weights to assign to various assets so as to achieve the maximum diversification for a given expected return. Portfolios that have this characteristic are deemed efficient, and a continuum of these portfolios plotted in dimensions of expected return and standard deviation form the efficient frontier. For this insight, Markowitz shared the 1990 Nobel Prize in economics.

One of the implementational challenges of portfolio selection is to estimate not just the volatilities of the assets in the portfolio but their correlations with each other as well. For example, a portfolio that comprises 100 assets requires 100 estimates of volatility and 4,050 estimates of correlation for a total of 5,050 risk estimates.

James Tobin, the 1981 winner of the Nobel prize in economics, showed that the investment process can be separated into two distinct steps:

1. The choice of a unique optimal portfolio along the efficient frontier

2. The decision to combine this portfolio with a riskless investment

This two step process is Tobin's famed separation theorem.[21]

Tobin showed that this unique portfolio along the efficient frontier, when combined with lending or borrowing at the riskless interest rate, dominates all other portfolios. Figure 6.1

---

[21] J. Tobin, "Liquidity Preferences as Behavior Towards Risk," *The Review of Economic Studies* (25th ed.) (February 1958), pp. 65–86.

Figure 6.1   Capital asset pricing model.

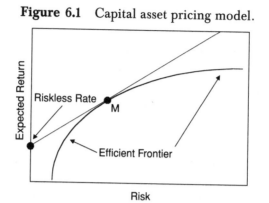

shows a two-dimensional graph, with risk represented by the horizontal axis and expected return represented by the vertical axis. Markowitz' efficient frontier appears as the positively sloped concave curve. The straight line emanating from the vertical axis at the riskless interest rate illustrates the efficient frontier with lending and borrowing. The segment between the riskless rate and the efficient frontier represents combinations of lending along with investment in the designated efficient portfolio. The continuation of this straight line beyond the efficient frontier represents combinations of borrowing along with investment in the designated efficient portfolio. Investors will prefer points along the straight line that is tangent to the efficient frontier at portfolio M, as long as investors can lend and borrow at the riskless interest rate and they have homogeneous views regarding expected returns, variances, and correlations.

William Sharpe, one of Markowitz' co-winners of the Nobel prize, extended Markowitz and Tobin's insights to develop a theory of market equilibrium under conditions of

Figure 6.2   Beta.

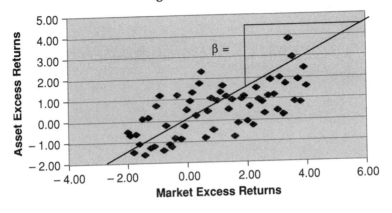

risk, which greatly reduced the number of risk estimates required for portfolio construction.[22]

Sharpe showed that portfolio M is the market portfolio of all risky assets, which represents the maximum achievable diversification. Moreover, he proceeded to show that risk can be partitioned into two sources—that caused by changes in the market portfolio, which cannot be diversified away, and that caused by nonmarket factors, which can be diversified away. He also showed that an asset's nondiversifiable risk is estimated by measuring how its excess return (its expected return less the riskless rate) changes for a given change in the market's excess return, as shown in Figure 6.2.

Figure 6.2 shows a scatter plot of returns. Each point represents combinations of the market's excess return and the asset's excess return for a given measurement period. The

---

[22] W. Sharpe, "Capital Asset Prices: A Theory of Market Equilibrium Under Conditions of Uncertainty," *Journal of Finance* (September 1964).

straight line passing through these points is the best fit of the data. Literally, it is the line that minimizes the aggregate magnitude of the deviations from it. The slope of this line, when squared and multiplied by the market's risk as measured by variance, quantifies the asset's nondiversifiable risk, and Sharpe called this slope beta. The deviations from the line represent risk that is specific to the individual asset and is diversified away in the market portfolio. In an efficient market, Sharpe argued that investors are only compensated for bearing risk that cannot be diversified away; thus, an asset's expected return, through its beta, is linearly related to the market's expected return.

Sharpe's model greatly reduces the number of risk parameters required for estimating a portfolio's risk. Instead of estimating 5,050 risk parameters to determine the risk of a 100 asset portfolio, we only need to estimate 101 risk parameters given the CAPM–the market's risk and the betas of the 100 assets.

Although Sharpe derived the notion of beta under conditions of market efficiency and equilibrium, it can be broadly applied to measure the relative risk of any asset with respect to a reference asset. From this relationship we can derive any asset's expected return given an assumption about a reference asset's expected return, including an option and its underlying asset. Specifically, an option's expected return equals:

$$R_o = \beta(R_A - R_R) + R_R$$

where R_O = Expected return of option

β = Beta of option with respect to underlying asset

R_A = Expected return of underlying asset

R_R = Riskless interest rate

With this brief detour, we are now prepared to estimate the option's expected return. We start by estimating the option's beta by relating the option's possible returns to the underlying asset's possible returns. In the event the stock increases 30% the option will be worth \$30. Its return, therefore, equals 30 minus its present value, all divided by its present value $[(30 - C_p)/C_p]$. However, we do not yet know its present value. That is the point of this whole exercise—to determine the option's present value. For now we must depict the option's return as a formula.

Let us now calculate the option's return in the event the stock declines 10%. If this happens the option will be worth nothing; thus its return conditioned on a 10% stock decline equals $(0 - C_p)/C_p$. Again, we must depict the option's return as a formula. The difference in the option's possible returns, therefore, equals $[(30 - C_p)/C_p] - [(0 - C_p)/C_p]$, which simplifies to $30/C_p$.

Now let us consider the possible stock returns. It either rises from \$100 to \$130 which produces a 30% return $[(130-100)/100]$, or it falls from \$100 to \$90 in which case its return equals -10% $[(90-100)/100]$; thus the difference in its possible returns is 40%.

Beta equals the difference in the option's excess returns given the stock's excess returns divided by the difference in the stock's excess returns. Because the riskless return is constant, beta will be the same whether we relate differences in excess returns or differences in total returns. Therefore, we calculate beta as $(30/C_p)/0.40$, which simplifies to $75/C_p$. Again, we must use a formula to represent beta because we do not yet know the option's present value.

In order to calculate the option's expected return, we simply substitute beta, along with the stock's expected return and the riskless rate, into Equation 6.1, as shown:

$$R_o = \left(\frac{75}{C_p}\right)(0.10 - 0.04) + 0.04$$

$$= \frac{75}{C_p}(0.06) + 0.04 \tag{6.1}$$

$$= \frac{4.5}{C_p} + 0.04$$

Now let us proceed to estimate the option's present value by discounting its expected ending value with the option's expected return rather the riskless interest rate. Its expected ending value, however, does not equal 35% of $30 but rather 50% of $30, because with an expected stock return of 10%, we implicitly assume a 50% probability that the option will be worth $30 at expiration. Thus the present value of the option equals $15 divided by one plus the option's expecte return or $15/[1 + (4.5/$C_p$ + 0.04)]. With some reasonably straightforward algebra, we again find that the option's present value equals $10.0962:

1. $C_p = \dfrac{15}{1 + (4.5/C_p + 0.04)}$

2. $C_p = \dfrac{15}{(1.04 + 4.5/C_p)}$

3. $C_p(1.04 + 4.5/C_p) = 15$

4. $1.04 C_p + 4.5 C_p / C_p = 15$

5. $1.04 C_p + 4.5 = 15$

6. $C_p = \dfrac{15 - 4.5}{1.04}$

7. $C_p = \dfrac{10.5}{1.04}$

8. $C_p = 10.0962$

The remarkable fact is that, even though we begin by discounting the option's true expected ending value of $15 by the option's true expected return, by step 7 it is apparent that this is equivalent to discounting its expected value under the assumption of risk neutrality ($10.5) by the riskless return. $10.5 is the option's expected ending value under the risk neutral assumption that there is only a 35% chance that the option will be worth $30. The value $4.5, therefore, represents the option's risk premium, and the algebra shows that it is subtracted from the option's true expected value, which enables us to use the riskless rate as the discount rate.

We have just seen that two ostensibly different valuation procedures are equivalent. In the first case, we assume that we can value an option as though we are indifferent to risk even though we are truly averse to risk. Under this assumption of risk neutrality, the expected ending value of the option is $10.50 ($0.35 \times 30). Risk neutrality allows us to use the riskless rate to derive the option's present value of $10.0962 ($10.50/1.04$).

In the second case, we assume that the expected ending value of the option equals $15 ($0.50 \times 30), and we derive an expected return for the option that is consistent with the stock's expected return of 10%. This derivation shows that the expected return of the option has a premium over the riskless return equal to $4.5/C_p$, which means that the premium varies with the unspecified present value of the option. By rearranging the terms to derive the option's present value, the premium in the option's expected return disappears and we are left with the riskless return as the discount rate. At the same time, the expected ending value of the option is reduced by 4.5, which results in precisely the same values we assumed under risk neutral valuation. This equivalence reveals the irrelevance of expected return:

$$C_p = \frac{15}{1.04 + 4.5/C_p} = \frac{15 - 4.5}{1.04} = \frac{10.5}{1.04}$$

I demonstrated this equivalence with a simple example of a stock that has only two possible outcomes. Nonetheless, the same equivalence applies to assets that have a wide, indeed infinite, number of possible ending values. We simply discount each possible ending option value by the riskless return and weight them according to their likelihood of occurrence to derive the option's present value. The beauty of risk neutral valuation is that even though we are truly risk averse and options are in fact risky, we can value them as though we are indifferent to their risk; hence the irrelevance of expected return.

THE BOTTOM LINE

- The Black-Scholes formula is the culmination of nearly 150 years of scientific inquiry, drawing on the achievements of several distinguished scientists from disparate fields.

Nobel Prize Winners and the Black-Scholes Formula

Albert Einstein (1921–physics). Einstein's work on Brownian motion produced an equation for the transfer of heat, which Black and Scholes used to derive their option formula.

Paul A. Samuelson (1970–economics). Samuelson's work on the valuation of warrants led to a formula of the same general form as the Black-Scholes formula, except that Samuelson used the expected return of the option as the drift term rather than the riskless return.

Franco Modigliani (1985–economics). Modigliani, along with Merton Miller, demonstrated the invariance of a firm's value to its capital structure and dividend policy, which paved the way for Black and Scholes to invoke the principles of no arbitrage to derive their formula.

Merton H. Miller (1990–economics). Miller, in addition to his work with Franco Modigliani, persuaded the *Journal of Political Economy* to publish the Black-Scholes manuscript.

Robert C. Merton (1997–economics). Merton introduced continuous time mathematics to finance, of which the Black-Scholes formula is the most famous example. He also gave Black and Scholes the key insight that if a hedged position is maintained continuously, its return becomes certain.

Myron Scholes (1997–economics). Scholes, along with Fischer Black, extended Merton's insight of a continuously maintained hedged position to set up a partial differential equation that is independent of investor risk preferences. The solution to this equation (from Einstein) is their celebrated option formula.

- The key innovation of the Black-Scholes formula is that the expected return of the underlying asset and, therefore, the expected return of the option itself, is irrelevant to the present value of the option.

- This irrelevance arises from the fact investors can construct hedged positions of the asset and the option, such that the asset's expected return offsets itself, rendering the hedged position riskless.

- Consequently, investors can value options as though they are indifferent to the option's risk, even though they are truly averse to it.

CHAPTER 7

Primer: Financial Concepts and Quantitative Methods

Finance is deceptively elegant. From simple notions we are able to derive remarkably profound results. Unfortunately, the path along the way is not always transparent. Many crucial steps are obscured because financial economists and mathematicians tend to depart from normal vernacular and lapse into a private dialect of technical jargon and symbolism. Ostensibly, they communicate this way because it promotes economy and exactitude, but a cynic might suspect that much of this rhetoric is used to enhance self-esteem. Sadly, the rest of us are too often left in the dark.

The purpose of this primer is to amend this situation, in at least a small way, by translating the recondite dialect of financial economists and mathematicians into terms that we all understand. This primer establishes a foundation of basic concepts and techniques to help us unravel the puzzles of finance. Let us therefore begin with one of the most basic terms–investment.

INVESTMENT

An investment is a resource that we do not consume. Obvious examples are savings accounts, bonds, and stocks. Real estate is less obvious. To the extent that it appreciates and generates income, real estate is certainly an investment. However, we consume our house, in part, by occupying it, so it has both investment attributes and consumption attributes.

Investments are not always financial in nature. Education is an investment in human capital. We forego consumption of leisure activities and defer employment in order to raise the value of our human capital. We accept this tradeoff because we expect eventually to exchange our human capital for future wealth or other nonfinancial reward. Therefore, investments have as their goal the production of wealth, either by generating ongoing income or by enhancing value which later can be exchanged for income.

However, not all investments produce income. We may choose to maintain an unnecessarily large balance in a non-interest bearing checking account. A checking account balance qualifies as an investment because we defer consumption, but we would not consider it a very sound investment.[1] In fact, after we account for the fact that prices rise, the return of a non-interest bearing checking account in a real sense is negative. We lose purchasing power. Moreover, we fail to capture the time value of money. Because a riskless investment such as a U.S. Treasury bill generates income even in the

---

[1] A minimal checking account balance is a sound investment because it yields convenience. This convenience yield is a form of nonfinancial income. A balance that exceeds the amount required for convenience is wasteful.

absence of inflation, time has value. Thus, we should require investments that have no risk to provide compensation for the time value of money and inflation. A risky investment should offer the expectation of additional return in the form of a risk premium to compensate for the uncertainty of its income stream and price at which it can be sold later.

RETURN

Return is expressed as a percentage of an investment's initial value, and it equals the income produced by the investment and its change in price over a specified period, all divided by the investment's price at the beginning of the period. For our purposes, we further qualify income to mean financial income. Therefore, our definition of investment return ignores the psychic income we may receive from owning a work of art or the utilitarian income we receive from occupying a house rather than renting it to others. The following equation describes investment return as a function of income and price change:

$$R = \frac{(I + P_E - P_B)}{P_B} \qquad (7.1)$$

where R = Return
$\quad I$ = Income
$\quad P_E$ = Ending price
$\quad P_B$ = Beginning price

Suppose we purchase 1,000 shares of a mutual fund that invests in common stock and that the price of a single share is $25.00. Our total purchase price is, therefore, $25,000.00.

We hold these shares for one year, during which time they each generate $0.75 in dividend income, which sums to $750.00. We now decide to sell them because the share price has risen in value to $30.00, and we believe the stock market has become overvalued. Our proceeds from the sale equal $30,000.00, which gives us a return of 23.00%, as shown:

$$\frac{(750.00 + 30,000.00 - 25,000.00)}{25,000.00} = 23.00\%$$

Our investment has produced $750.00 of income and a capital gain from its change in price of $5,000.00, which together equals 23.00% of its initial value.

Now consider the return of an investment over several years. Suppose we shift our proceeds of $30,750.00 to a mutual fund that specializes in bonds, with an initial share value of $15.00. We thus acquire 2,050 shares of this bond fund (30,750/15 = 2,050). Suppose that interest income is distributed annually at the end of the year and that we purchase additional shares with this interest income; that is, we reinvest the income. Table 7.1 shows how the value of this fund grows from year to year and the resultant annual rates of return.

In the first year, our bond fund generates $1,845.00 of interest income, but its share value declines to $13.85 (more precisely, $13.846154). Thus the value of our original 2,050 shares is $28,384.62. However, we acquire 133.25 new shares which brings our total to 2,183.25 (1,845.00/13.85 + 2050.00 = 2,183.25). At year-end these shares are worth $30,229.62. Referring to Equation 7.1 we compute the first year's return to equal:

$$\frac{(1,845.00 + 28,384.62 - 30,750.00)}{30,750.00} = -1.69\%$$

Table 7.1 Annual total return.

Year	Beginning Share Value	Beginning Number of Shares	Beginning Fund Value	Interest Income	Ending Share Value	Shares Purchased	Ending Number of Shares	Ending Fund Value	Annual Total Return (%)
1	15.00	2,050.00	30,750.00	1,845.00	13.85	133.25	2,183.25	30,229.62	−1.69
2	13.85	2,183.25	30,229.62	1,964.93	15.25	128.81	2,312.06	35,268.74	16.67
3	15.25	2,312.06	35,268.74	2,080.86	16.36	127.16	2,439.23	39,914.59	13.17
4	16.36	2,439.23	39,914.59	2,195.30	16.07	136.60	2,575.82	41,397.14	3.71
5	16.07	2,575.82	41,397.14	2,318.24	16.67	139.09	2,714.92	45,248.60	9.30

A more succinct way to compute total return, when the ending value already encompasses the reinvested income, is to divide the ending value by the beginning value and then to subtract 1 to separate the incremental part of the ratio, as given by Equation 7.2:

$$R = \frac{V_E}{V_B} - 1 \qquad (7.2)$$

where R = Return
V_E = Ending value
V_B = Beginning value

therefore,

$$\frac{30,229.62}{30,750.00} - 1 = -1.69\%$$

Equation 7.2 simply gives the percentage change in our fund's value, which is equivalent to total return as long as the ending value includes all of the income that was generated during the period. I have switched from "price" to "value" in Equation 7.2 to emphasize that, unlike in the first example, the investments in our fund need not be sold in order to calculate total return. Value represents the price at which the investments could be sold and should equal price precisely in perfectly liquid markets. The fact that the investments are not necessarily sold is immaterial to the calculation of total return. Our gains or losses are unrealized as opposed to realized. If, however, their recorded values differ from the prices at which we could actually transact, our calculation only approximates the true but unobservable total return. More likely total return would be lower owing to the fact that we would be forced to accept a lower price when selling into an illiquid market and to pay a higher price when purchasing assets in an illiquid market.

Now consider the cumulative return over all five periods. One way to calculate this return is to apply Equation 7.2 to the value at the beginning of the five year period and the value at the end of the period, which results in a cumulative total five-year return of 47.15% (45,248.60/30,750.00 − 1 = 0.4715). Alternatively, we can link the annual returns.

Linking essentially reinvests each prior gain or loss, including income, in the subsequent period's return. For example, we started our investment in the bond fund with an initial contribution of $30,750.00. This investment lost 1.69% in the first period, which corresponds to a dollar loss of $520.38 (30,750.00 × −1.69% = −520.38). Therefore, the amount that is left to invest in the second period's return equals $30,229.62. Keep in mind that the $520.38 loss combines both the interest income generated by our investment plus the capital loss that it incurred.

We are more fortunate in the second period, because the fund's total return equals 16.67% (more precisely, 16.6695%), which generates a dollar gain of $5,039.12 (30,229.62 × 16.67% = 5,039.12). We can also compute this gain by subtracting the fund's value at the beginning of period 2 from its ending value that period (35,268.74 − 30,229.62 = 5,039.12).

In the third period we invest the amount we began with in the second period, $30,229.62, plus the gain in the second period, $5,039.12, which collectively returns 13.17%.

In each period we apply the total return, reflecting both income and capital gains or losses, to the fund's value at the beginning of the period. This reinvestment of the fund's return each period is called compounding. Because we only reinvest once per year, we are compounding annually. This process results in Equation 7.3 for computing cumulative return from a sequence of periodic returns:[2]

$$R_C = (1 + R_1) \times (1 + R_2) \times (1 + R_3 \times \cdots \times (1 + R_n) - 1 \qquad (7.3)$$

where R_C = Cumulative return
      $R_{1 \ldots n}$ = Periodic returns in periods 1 through n

Let us apply Equation 7.3 to the annual returns shown in Table 7.1:

$$(1 + (-1.69\%)) \times (1 + 16.67\%) \times (1 + 13.17\%) \times (1 + 3.71\%)$$
$$\times (1 + 9.30\%) - 1 = 47.15\%$$

Equation 7.3 normalizes or scales the initial value to 1.00 and then invests this value at the first rate of return—in our example, 1.00 times $[1 + (-1.69\%)]$—which yields 0.9831.[3] This value represents the same percentage decrease from 1.00 as 30,229.62 does from 30,750.00. The equation then invests 0.9831 at the second rate of return, 0.9831 times (1 + 16.67%). The 1s that are added to the rates of return preserve the values at the start of each period. In other words, we receive 100.00% of the value we start with plus an incremental component of 16.67%. For example, after the second period, we multiply 1 times 0.9831 (to preserve the 0.9831) plus 16.67% times 0.9831 (to apply the period's return),

---

[2] I use the term, periodic return, to refer to the percentage change of an investment's value over a given period, assuming its income has been reinvested.

[3] The initial value of 1.00 does not appear in the equation. It is only implied because multiplying by 1 does not change the result.

which we represent more succinctly as 1.1667 times 0.9831. This calculation leads to our investment's value at the end of the second period, $35,268.74. The quantities, 1 plus each period's rate of return, are called "wealth relatives." By multiplying these wealth relatives together, we arrive at a factor, which when multiplied by our investment's initial value, yields its ending value. Because we normalize the beginning value to equal 1.00 when we link returns, by subtracting 1 from the product of the wealth relatives, we end up with the cumulative return. In other words, 1.4715 equals the same percentage difference from 1.00 as does 45,258.60 from 30,750.00. The value of this approach is that we do not need to know the beginning or ending value of our investment. We simply need to know its periodic returns, which often times is all the information we have.

Equation 7.4 uses mathematical notation to abbreviate Equation 7.3:

$$R_C = \prod_{i=1}^{n}(1+R_i)-1 \qquad (7.4)$$

where R_C = Cumulative return
R_i = Periodic returns in periods i through n

Π is a mathematical symbol which indicates that the terms in the parentheses are to be multiplied. R takes on whatever value is associated with period i, starting with period 1 and proceeding through period n, which is a generic symbol for the final period. In our prior example, when $i = 1$, $R = -1.69\%$, and when $i = 2$, $R = 16.67\%$; hence the equation calls for us to multiply together, the quantities, 1 plus each of the periods' returns through $i = 5$ when $R = 9.30\%$, and then to subtract 1. It instructs us to perform the same operations as Equation 7.3, but its instructions are presented more succinctly.

ANNUALIZATION

It is often convenient to express a cumulative result as an annualized value; that is, the return which when repeated yearly, aggregates to the cumulative multiyear return. Our first instinct might be simply to divide the cumulative return by the number of years in the multiyear period. This value is called the arithmetic average or the mean, and in our bond fund it equals 9.43% $(47.15\%/5 = 9.43\%)$. Let us see what happens when we invest each year at this average rate of return by substituting 9.43% for the actual periodic returns in Equation 7.3.

$$(1 + 9.43\%) \times (1 + 9.43\%) \times (1 + 9.43\%) \times (1 + 9.43\%)$$
$$\times (1 + 9.43\%) - 1 = 56.92\%$$

When we link, or equivalently, compound forward at the arithmetic average, we end up with a higher cumulative return than the periodic returns actually produced. This overestimation of the cumulative return occurs because the arithmetic average does not assume that the component returns are compounded; rather it assumes they are summed. The constant rate of return associated with compounding is called the geometric average return, and it equals 8.03% in our example.

When we are dealing with a constant rate of return that we wish to compound forward, we can employ a short cut.

Raising a number to a power is equivalent to multiplying that number by itself as many times as represented by the power. For example, 10^2 equals 10×10, and 1.10^3 equals $1.10 \times 1.10 \times 1.10$. Therefore, with a slight modification to Equation 7.3 we can derive the geometric average from a sequence of periodic returns. We wish to know which rate of return, when substituted for the actual periodic returns, yields a cumulative return of 47.15%. Thus we begin by setting the following expression equal to $1 + 47.15\%$:

$$(1+R_G)\times(1+R_G)\times(1+R_G)\times(1+R_G)\times(1+R_G)=1+47.15\%$$

Because 1.4715 is the product of 1 plus the geometric average, $(1+R_G)$, multiplied by itself five times or equivalently $(1+R_G)^5$, we solve for $(1+R_G)$ by raising 1 plus the cumulative return to the $\frac{1}{5}$ power; that is, $(1+R_C)^{\frac{1}{5}}$. This value equals 1.0803. We then subtract the 1 that we added to 47.15% to arrive at 8.03%.

Our earlier estimate of 9.43%, the arithmetic average of the sequence of returns, is the geometric average of 56.92%. The fact that it exceeds the corresponding geometric average of the returns for which it is the arithmetic average is an important relationship in finance. Unless all of the periodic returns are identical to each other, and therefore the arithmetic and geometric averages are equal, the arithmetic average will always exceed the geometric average. Under no circumstances will it be lower than the geometric average. When the periodic returns are equal to one another, the arithmetic average will equal the geometric average.[4]

---

[4] The geometric average return is approximately equal to the arithmetic average return less $\frac{1}{2}$ the variance of periodic returns.

Equation 7.4 defines cumulative return as a function of the geometric average, whereas Equation 7.6 shows how the geometric average is derived from the cumulative return:

$$R_C = (1 + R_G)^n - 1 \qquad (7.5)$$

$$R_G = (1 + R_C)^{1/n} - 1 \qquad (7.6)$$

where R_C = Cumulative return
R_G = Geometric average return
n = Number of periods

MANIPULATION

Yes, the heading for this section is intended as a double entendre. Equations 7.1 through 7.6 enable us to manipulate (constructively) the return of any periodicity into its components or its aggregate. They also allow investment advisors to manipulate (deceptively) a return into a technically correct but often misleading corresponding return that presents their performance in a more favorable light. I will focus on positive applications of these equations, but briefly mention a common investment advisor ploy.

Over six years our investment has appreciated, through income and change in value, from $25,000.00 to $45,248.60. It generated 23.00% for one year while it was invested in stocks, and then 47.15% over five years during which time it was invested in bonds. What has been its cumulative return over the entire six-year period? Equation 7.2 provides one approach for answering this question. We simply divide 45,248.60 by 25,000.00 and subtract 1, which yields a cumulative return of

80.99%. Alternatively, we can apply Equation 7.3 and multiply the wealth relative of the cumulative stock return by the wealth relative of the cumulative bond return and subtract 1. We are not restricted to using annual returns when multiplying wealth relatives together:

$$(1.2300 \times 1.4715) - 1 = 0.8099$$

Happily, both approaches yield the same answer. Now suppose we wish to calculate the geometric average of our six-year investment. We simply apply Equation 7.6 to the six-year cumulative return:

$$(1 + 0.8099)^{1/6} - 1 = 0.1039$$

Thus, the annualized return (geometric average) for the past six-years is 10.39%. If we had invested $25,000.00 in a fund that returned 10.39% annually, and we reinvested the yearly gains, our fund's value would have grown to the same $45,248.60.

Suppose we now wish to calculate the annual return that is required in order for our fund's value to grow to $75,000.00 during the next four years. We divide 75,000.00 by 45,248.60, raise this value to the 1/4 power and then subtract 1. This procedure yields an annualized return of 13.47%.

From this result we can calculate the annualized return required to increase $25,000.00 to $75,000.00 over 10 years. It is computed as $(1.1039^6 \times 1.1347^4)^{1/10} - 1$, which equals 11.61%.

This corresponds to a 10-year cumulative return of 200.00%. We could have calculated this cumulative return by dividing $75,000.00 by $25,000.00 and subtracting 1, and then annualized it by raising $(1.00 + 2.00)$ to the 1/10 power and subtracting 1 $(3.00^{1/10} - 1 = 0.1161)$.

These calculations show how easy it is to manipulate returns once we know either the beginning and ending values or the periodic returns. When measuring performance, it is quite reasonable to convert a multi-period return to its sub-period constant return, such as converting a 200.00% 10-year cumulative return to an annualized 11.61% return. We might even want to convert the annualized return to a constant quarterly return, by raising 1.1161 to the 1/4 power or by raising 3.00 to the 1/40 power (there are 40 quarters in a 10-year period). These calculations show that the quarterly return equals 2.78%, which implies that a constant return of 2.78% compounded quarterly over 10 years raises a $25,000.00 initial investment to $75,000.00. It also implies that 2.78% compounded quarterly results in an annual return of 11.61%.

It is inappropriate, however, to extrapolate a subperiod return to its corresponding multiperiod return, when measuring historical performance. If after one quarter, for example, we produced a 2.78% rate of return, it would be misleading to report this as an annualized return of 11.61%, because it implicitly forecasts that we will continue to perform at a quarterly return of 2.78%. Investment advisors sometimes annualize subannual results to create the illusion of higher returns, given that some customers often overlook details. If over a full year, however, we achieved an 11.61% return, converting it to its quarterly equivalent is simply a statement of fact. It is not a forecast of continued favorable returns.

CONTINUOUS RETURN

The frequency with which a return is compounded has important implications for financial analysis. Consider, for example, a hypothetical investment that returns 100% per year. Granted, this example is unrealistic, but it will serve to illustrate one of the most important and useful results in financial analysis. If we invest $1.00 for one year (again, an unrealistic but convenient assumption) with no compounding, at the end of the year our investment will grow to $2.00. Suppose instead that the return is compounded semi-annually; that is, our investment increases at a rate of 50% for the first six months at which point our $1.00 investment equals $1.50. Then this amount grows at 50% for the next six months, which leads to a final value of $2.25 (1.00 × 1.50 = 1.50 × 1.50 = 2.25). Table 7.2 reveals what happens when we continually raise the frequency at which we compound.

Table 7.2 reveals that future value increases with more frequent compounding, but at a slower and slower rate and, of critical importance, up to a limit. Irrespective of how often we compound, $1.00 invested at an annualized rate of

Table 7.2 One dollar invested at 100% compounded forward at increasing frequencies.

Frequency of Compounding	Number of Periods	Compounded Future Value
Semi-annually	2	2.25000000
Quarterly	4	2.44140625
Monthly	12	2.61303529
Weekly	52	2.69259695
Daily	365	2.71456748
Hourly	8,760	2.71812669
Per minute	525,600	2.71827924
Per second	31,536,000	2.71828178
Per 100th second	3,153,600,000	2.71828166
Continuously	Infinite	2.71828183

100.00% will never grow to more than $2.72 in a single year (more precisely, more than 2.718282). The value 2.718282, which is denoted by *e,* is the base of the natural logarithm. It is literally the limit of Equation 7.7 when the annualized rate of return equals 100.00% and the frequency of compounding approaches infinity:

$$FV = (1 + r/n)^n \qquad (7.7)$$

where *FV* = Future value
     r = Annualized return
     n = Frequency of compounding

Consider semiannual compounding when the annualized return equals 100.00%. The future value equals 2.25 $((1 + 100\%/2)^2 = 2.25)$. As *n* increases, the future value from Equation 7.7 approaches 2.718282.

The value *e* has special properties. When *e* is raised to an exponent equal to a continuous return, and then multiplied by the beginning value, it yields the ending value that comes from continuously compounding the beginning value forward at that return. Before we explore this result, let us digress briefly to review logarithms, since *e* is defined as the base of the natural logarithm.

The logarithm of a particular value is the exponent, which when a base is raised to that exponent, results in that value. For example, the logarithm of 100 to the base 10 equals 2, because $10^2 = 100$. Similarly, the logarithm of 1,000 to the base 10 equals 3 $(10^3 = 1,000)$. In the early days of finance, logarithms were thought to be convenient because, with an implement called a slide rule, they allowed multiplication by addition. For example, we can multiply 100 by

1,000 by summing their logarithms and then raising base 10 to the sum of their respective logarithms ($10^2 \times 10^3 \times 10^{2+3} = 10^5 = 100,000$). We do not need logarithms to multiply 100 by 1,000, but if we knew the logarithms of other large values that were not nice round numbers, it might be more convenient to sum their logarithms with a slide rule to arrive at their product than to multiply the values. The fact that logarithms are summed to generate the product of their corresponding numbers is critical to financial analysis, as we will see later. Now let us return to e and its relationship to continuous returns.

When e is raised to a continuous return, it yields 1 plus the periodic return. By multiplying this quantity by a beginning investment value, we derive the continuously compounded value of that investment.

For example, suppose we wish to know to what value $25,000.00 will grow after one year if it is invested at a continuously compounded return of 20.70%. We simply multiply $25,000.00 by $e^{0.2070}$, which equals $30,750.00. Thus 20.70% is the corresponding continuous return of 23.00% [$(30,750 / 25,000) -1 = 23.00\%$]. If we had invested $25,000 in a fund with a continuously compounded return of 20.70%, it would have generated the same value after one year as our stock fund that produced a periodic return of 23.00%. It thus follows that the natural logarithm of 1.23 equals 20.70%.

If the relationship between e, continuous returns, and natural logarithms is not yet clear, it might be helpful to revisit our earlier example of the value 1.00 compounded forward continuously at a rate of 100.00%. It results in a value equal to 1.00 plus 171.8282%, or 2.718282. Thus 100% is the corresponding continuous return of the periodic return, 171.8282%, and it is equal to the natural logarithm of

$(1 + 171.8282\%)$. The following expressions summarize the relationship between e and the natural logarithm, which is usually abbreviated by ln.

$$\left(\frac{1+100\%}{n}\right)^n = 2.718282$$

As n approaches infinity

$$e^{100\%} = 2.718282$$
$$ln(1 + 171.8282\%) = ln(2.718282) = ln(e) = 100\%$$

These relationships allow us to convert any periodic return into its continuous return by taking the natural logarithm of the quantity, 1 plus the periodic return. For example, the corresponding continuous return of a 10.00% periodic return equals $ln(1.10)$ which is 9.53%. By symmetry, if we compound continuously for one year at 9.53%, our periodic return for the year equals 10.00% ($e^{0.093} - 1 = 10.00\%$), and it follows that an initial investment of $25,000.00 compounded continuously at 9.53% for one year appreciates to $27,500.00 ($25,000.00 \times e^{0.093} = 27,500.00$).

To summarize:

- $ln(1 + \text{periodic return}) = \text{Continuous return}$
- $e^{\text{continuous return}} = 1 + \text{Periodic return}$
- $e^{\text{continuous return}} - 1 = \text{Periodic return}$
- Beginning value $\times$ $e^{\text{continuous return}} = \text{Ending value}$

By now, it should be apparent that e is a very handy number. It will appear time and again along with ln, the

More about *e*

The value *e* has a remarkable number of connections to seemingly disparate natural, manmade, and mathematical phenomena:

- The ability to perceive increments of pain, weight, and musical pitch are all functions of *e*.

- Many patterns in nature, including the growth pattern of shells, tusks, sunflowers, and even galaxies are related to *e*.

- The curvature of the Gateway Arch in St. Louis is described by a function based on *e*.

- If four bugs are placed at the corners of a square and at the same time, each bug moves toward its neighbor, they will trace a pattern to the center of the square that is a function of *e*.

- *e* equals $1 + 1/1! + 1/2! + 1/3! + 1/4! + 1/5! + \ldots$

- *e* is part of the most elegant equation in mathematics: $e^{\Pi i} + 1 = 0$, where *i* is the imaginary number $\sqrt{-1}$ and Π equals the constant $3.14\ldots$

- Finally, *e* is related to the Prime Number Theorem, which gives the probability that a particular integer is a prime number.

---

*For those who wish to learn more about *e*, I recommend a marvelously entertaining book by Eli Maor called, *e: The Story of a Number* (Princeton, NJ: Princeton University Press, 1994). These observations are taken from Maor's wonderful book.

symbol for the natural logarithm, as we decipher the puzzles of finance.

CONTINUOUS RETURNS AND THE GEOMETRIC AVERAGE

Before we move on to risk, it will be useful to explore one more aspect of return; that is, the relationship between continuous returns and the geometric average return. Table 7.3 illustrates how they are related.

The first column in Table 7.3 shows the annual returns generated by our bond investment. The next column adds one to these returns to produce their respective wealth relatives. The third column shows the cumulative value of $1.00 each period, which is derived by multiplying together the wealth relatives as demonstrated by Equation 7.3. If we raise 1.4715, the cumulative value after five years, to the 1/5th power and then subtract 1 from it, we arrive at

Table 7.3 Relationship between continuous returns and geometric average.

Year	Periodic Returns (%)	Wealth Relatives	Cumulative Value of $1	Continuous Returns (%)
1	−1.69	0.9831	0.9831	−1.71
2	16.67	1.1667	1.1470	15.42
3	13.17	1.1317	1.2980	12.37
4	3.71	1.0371	1.3462	3.65
5	9.30	1.0930	1.4715	8.90
Geometric average of periodic returns $(1.4715^{1/5} - 1)$				8.03
Arithmetic average of continuous returns				7.73
Natural logarithm of 1 + Geometric average $[ln(1.0803)]$				7.73

the geometric average of 8.03%. The final column shows the continuous returns that correspond to the periodic returns. They are calculated as the natural logarithms of the wealth relatives. The arithmetic average of these continuous returns equals 7.73%. It is calculated simply by summing the five continuous returns and then dividing this sum by five. The arithmetic average of continuous returns is critical to the solution of many financial problems. Table 7.3 reveals an interesting and extremely convenient fact. The natural logarithm of the quantity, 1 plus the geometric average, is identical to the arithmetic average of the corresponding continuous returns:

$$ln(1 + R_G) = \frac{(R_{C1} + R_{C2} + R_{C3} + \cdots R_{Cn})}{n}$$

RISK

Financial risk represents the likelihood of experiencing an unpleasant investment outcome such as a significant loss or failure to achieve an expected gain. In this section we derive a risk measurement system from one simple assumption; that an investment either generates a particular gain with probability p or a particular loss with probability $1-p$. Table 7.4 shows the cumulative effect of this assumption extended over six periods for a $1,000.00 initial investment with an equal probability of a 25% gain or a 5% loss over a single period.

Altogether, there are 64 possible paths $(2^6 = 64)$ that lead to seven different values after six periods. In general, the number of ending values for a binomial process equals 2

Table 7.4 Distribution of ending values after six periods: Equal probability of 25 percent increase or 5 percent decrease.

Starting Value	Values after Period						Geometric Return (%)
	1	2	3	4	5	6	
						3,814.70	25.00
					3,051.76		
				2,441.41		2,899.17	19.41
			1,953.13		2,319.34		
		1,562.50		1,855.47		2,203.37	14.07
	1,250.00		1,484.38		1,762.70		
1,000.00		1,187.50		1,410.16		1,674.56	8.97
	950.00		1,128.13		1,339.65		
		902.50		1,071.72		1,272.67	4.10
			857.38		1,018.13		
				814.51		967.23	−0.55
					773.78		
						735.09	−5.00

raised to the number of iterations. One possible path, for example, is a succession of six straight 25% increases, which leads to an ending value of $3,814.70. This sequence is the only path that leads to this ending value. Therefore, the probability of this ending value equals 1.56% (1/64 = 1.56%). The next best outcome would be an ending value of $2,899.17. There are six paths that lead to this value:

+25%, +25%, +25%, +25%, +25%, −5%

+25%, +25%, +25%, +25%, −5%, +25%

+25%, +25%, +25%, −5%, +25%, +25%

+25%, +25%, −5%, +25%, +25%, +25%

+25%, −5%, +25%, +25%, +25%, +25%

−5%, +25%, +25%, +25%, +25%, +25%

Thus, the likelihood of achieving this result equals 9.38% (6/64 = 9.38%). Table 7.5 shows the number of paths leading to each of the seven ending values, their associated geometric returns, their relative frequencies, and their cumulative probabilities.

The information presented in Table 7.5 describes the riskiness of this investment because it conveys the magnitude of a potential loss and the likelihood of experiencing a loss or failing to achieve a particular gain. For example, of the 64 possible paths, 57 of them result in gains, while seven of the paths lead to losses. Thus we infer that this investment after six periods has an 89% (57/64 = 89%) chance of producing a gain and only an 11% (7/64 = 11%) chance of generating a loss. This probability of loss is also apparent from the cumulative probability column, which shows that all of the paths resulting in gains collectively have a cumulative probability of 89%.

Table 7.5 Relative frequency of paths.

Ending Values	Geometric Return (%)	Number of Paths	Relative Frequency (%)	Cumulative Probability (%)
3,814.70	25.00	1	1.56	1.56
2,899.17	19.41	6	9.38	10.94
2,203.37	14.07	15	23.44	34.38
1,674.56	8.97	20	31.25	65.63
1,272.67	4.10	15	23.44	89.06
967.23	−0.55	6	9.38	98.44
735.09	−5.00	1	1.56	100.00

THE NORMAL DISTRIBUTION

One of the most profound results in statistics is revealed by extending the number of periods for this investment. After one period, there is an equal chance of experiencing a 25% gain or losing 5%. When all of the outcomes have an equal chance of occurrence they are said to be uniformly distributed. This is the case for our investment after one period. After two periods, however, our investment is twice as likely to achieve the middle return because there are two paths that achieve this return. Thus the returns are no longer uniformly distributed. Figure 7.1 displays the probability for each geometric return after two periods.

As we increase the number of periods over which we compound our investment, the distribution of returns forms a very particular pattern. From the extreme returns on either side, the probability of occurrence increases, first at an increasing rate and then at a decreasing rate, as the returns

Figure 7.1 Distribution of geometric returns after two periods.

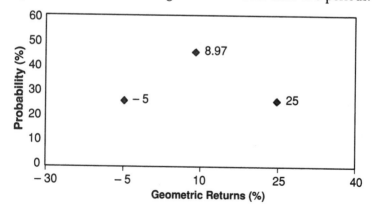

approach the central return, as shown in Figure 7.2. The returns are connected by a line to highlight this pattern.

This process is true when probable outcomes are averaged or summed. We would observe the same pattern if we recorded the average or sum of the values that resulted from multiple tosses of larger and larger numbers of dice. For example, multiple tosses of one die generate a uniform distribution because each side of the die is equally likely. Multiple tosses of two dice, however, would produce more averages clustered around the value 3.5 than at 1 or 6. As we increase the number of dice to a very larger number the distribution of the average outcome conforms to a bell shaped curve or, more precisely, a normal distribution. The same is true as we increase the number of periods over which we invest—almost. This "almost" is a critical qualification.

If you are unusually perceptive, you will notice that the distribution in Figure 7.2 is slightly skewed. Specifically, the occurrences toward the right end of the distribution stretch

Figure 7.2 Distribution of geometric returns after six periods.

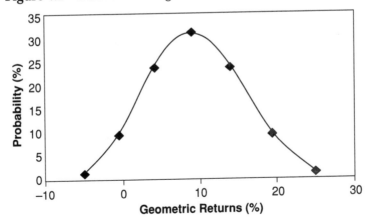

further to the right than those on the left stretch to the left. This skewness results from compounding. A 15% above average return compounded over multiple periods produces a geometric average return that is 16.03% above the middle geometric average return whereas a 15% below average return compounded over multiple periods produces a geometric average return that is only 13.97% below the middle geometric average return. Table 7.6 shows this asymmetry in terms of the geometric returns, cumulative returns, and ending values.

Thus far we have seen that random processes, which individually generate equally likely outcomes, such as the toss of die, when aggregated, produce a normal distribution of results. Normal distributions have wonderfully convenient properties, one of which is symmetry. We will soon investigate symmetry and other properties of the normal distribution. But first we must address the asymmetric or non-normal distribution that arises from compounding equally likely returns.

We would like a measure of return that is normally distributed so that we can invoke the properties of the normal

Table 7.6 Asymmetry from compounding.

Geometric Returns (%)	Distance from Middle Value (%)	Cumulative Returns (%)	Distance from Middle Value (%)	Ending Values	Distance from Middle Value
25.00	16.03	281.47	214.04	3,814.70	2,140.36
19.41	10.44	189.90	122.46	2,898.97	1,224.64
14.07	5.10	120.31	52.87	2,203.07	528.74
8.97	0.00	67.43	0.00	1,674.33	0.00
4.10	−4.87	27.26	−40.17	1,272.64	−401.70
−0.55	−9.52	−3.25	−70.69	967.45	−706.88
−5.00	−13.97	−26.49	−93.92	735.09	−939.24

distribution to measure risk. We use the continuous return because we sum these values to arrive at a cumulative result whereas we multiply periodic returns to generate a cumulative result.

Figure 7.3 shows the distribution of the corresponding continuous returns associated with our six period investment. Again, if you are unusually perceptive, you will notice that the distribution of continuous returns is precisely symmetric. Those of you with normal perceptive abilities can use Table 7.7 to confirm this symmetry.

If we were to repeat our investment over a very large number of periods, the distribution of the associated continuous returns would not only be symmetric, but as mentioned earlier, it would be normal. At this point you may be tempted to say, "so what?" Investments do not typically have an equal probability of a 25% increase or a 5% loss. However, the same pattern of possible paths generated by repeating the investment over more and more periods in which it either

Figure 7.3   Distribution of continuous returns after six periods.

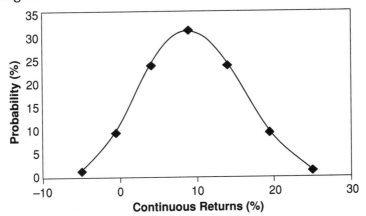

Table 7.7 Symmetry of continuous returns.

Continuous Returns (%)	Distance from Middle Value (%)
22.31	13.72
17.74	9.15
13.17	4.57
8.59	0.00
4.02	−4.57
−0.56	−9.15
−5.13	−13.72

increases 25% or decreases 5% is also obtained by dividing a single period into many finer and finer intervals with proportionally smaller gains or losses. This is reality. At any instant in time an investment such as a stock or bond might increase a tiny discrete amount or fall by a slight fraction. The accumulation of these very small discrete changes into daily, weekly, monthly, quarterly, annual, or any periodicity of returns results in a normal distribution of the corresponding continuous returns even if the small discrete returns are not equally likely to occur. Therefore, the corresponding continuous returns of an investment's historical periodic returns are well approximated by a normal distribution.

Normality has several convenient features that enable us to measure an investment's risk. The mean (or average), which is the expected value, the median, which is the middle value, and the mode, which is the most common value, are all equal to one another. Moreover, we can infer the entire distribution from only two values, the mean and the variance. Whereas the mean, along with the median and mode, measures the central tendency of the distribution, the variance measures the dispersion of the distribution.

Variance is equal to the average of the squared differences of each of the returns from the mean return, as shown in Equation 7.8 or more succinctly in Equation 7.9:

$$\sigma_C^2 = \frac{[(R_{C1} - \mu_C)^2 + (R_{C2} - \mu_C)^2 + (R_{C3} - \mu_C)^2 + \cdots + (R_{Cn} - \mu_C)^2]}{n} \quad (7.8)$$

$$\sigma_C^2 = \frac{\sum_{i=1}^{n}(R_{Ci} - \mu_C)^2}{n} \quad (7.9)$$

where σ_C^2 = Variance of continuous returns
R_{Ci} = Continuous return in period i
μ_C = Mean (arithmetic average) of continuous returns
n = Number of continuous returns

The Greek symbol Σ, which is called sigma, serves a similar function as Π does in Equation 7.4, except it instructs us to sum the differences from the mean of the continuous returns rather than to multiply them. Although variance measures dispersion, it does so in squared units because all the differences are squared. Squaring is necessary to prevent the differences from canceling each other out. It is common to re-state dispersion in the same units as the original data by taking the square root of the variance. This measure of dispersion is called the standard deviation.

$$\sigma_C = \sqrt{\sigma_C^2} \quad (7.10)$$

where σ_C = Standard deviation of continuous returns

Table 7.8 shows the computation of the variance and standard deviation from the quarterly returns produced by our bond investment. You may wish to verify that these quarterly returns compounded forward yield the annual returns displayed in Tables 7.1 and 7.3.

Table 7.8 shows the mean, variance, and standard deviation of the continuous returns that correspond to the quarterly

Table 7.8 Variance and standard deviation.

| Quarter | Quarterly | | Difference from Mean (%) | Squared Difference (%) |
	Periodic Return (%)	Continuous Return (%)		
1	0.11	0.11	−1.82	0.03
2	3.22	3.17	1.24	0.02
3	−2.13	−2.15	−4.08	0.17
4	−2.79	−2.83	−4.76	0.23
5	3.11	3.06	1.13	0.01
6	2.45	2.42	0.49	0.00
7	−1.09	−1.10	−3.03	0.09
8	11.66	11.03	9.10	0.83
9	5.32	5.18	3.25	0.11
10	4.43	4.33	2.40	0.06
11	−0.12	−0.12	−2.05	0.04
12	3.02	2.98	1.05	0.01
13	1.12	1.11	−0.82	0.01
14	3.21	3.16	1.23	0.02
15	0.55	0.55	−1.38	0.02
16	−1.17	−1.17	−3.11	0.10
17	2.45	2.42	0.49	0.00
18	6.52	6.32	4.38	0.19
19	−3.21	−3.26	−5.19	0.27
20	3.48	3.42	1.49	0.02
Mean of continuous returns				1.93
Variance (mean of squared differences)				0.11
Standard deviation (square root of variance)				3.33

periodic returns. If we assume that these values are representative of the central tendency and dispersion of future quarterly returns, and if we accept the theoretical result demonstrated earlier that continuous returns are normally distributed, we are able to infer the likelihood of achieving or failing to achieve any return.

For example, the normal distribution has the property that 68% of its values fall within plus and minus one standard deviation of its mean. Thus slightly more than 2/3 of our bond investment's future returns should be between −1.40% (1.93% − 3.33%) and 5.26% (1.93% + 3.33%). It follows, therefore, that there is a 16% chance of experiencing a quarterly return of less than −1.40%, because 32% of the distribution lies outside of the one standard deviation range. Half of this 32% is to the left of the one standard deviation range and half is to the right. These returns are measured as continuous returns. If we are interested in the one standard deviation range of periodic returns, we simply convert −1.40% and 5.26% to their periodic equivalents by raising e to the power −1.40% and 5.26%, respectively and then subtracting 1:

$$e^{-0.0140} - 1 = -1.39\%$$

$$e^{0.0526} - 1 = 5.40\%$$

Thus, there is a 16% chance of experiencing a quarterly periodic return that is less than −1.39% or greater than 5.40%.

By extending the range around the mean to plus and minus two standard deviations, we capture 95% of the returns under the normal distribution. Hence, our bond investment has a 2.50% chance of experiencing a quarterly periodic return that is less than −4.62% $\left(e^{(0.0193 - 2 \times 0.0333)} - 1\right)$ or greater than 8.97% $\left(e^{(0.0193 + 2 \times 0.0333)} - 1\right)$.

The relevant point is that we can express any area under the normal distribution as the mean plus or minus a particular number of standard deviation units. Moreover, because an area under the normal distribution is exactly equivalent to a probability of occurrence, an investment's standard deviation, in combination with its mean, provides an excellent summary of its riskiness.

SUMMARY

To summarize the concepts reviewed in this primer:

- An investment is a resource that we do not consume.

- Most investments have positive expected returns to compensate for the time value of money, inflation, and risk in the case of an uncertain income stream and future value.

- Periodic return is equal to the change in value of an investment plus the income it generates, expressed as a percentage of its beginning value.

- Wealth relatives are equal to 1 plus the periodic returns and are used to compute cumulative return.

- We calculate an investment's cumulative return by multiplying together each period's wealth relative and then subtracting 1.

- The geometric average return is a constant periodic rate of return, which when compounded forward periodically, yields the cumulative return derived from the actual periodic returns.

- The continuous return is a constant rate of return which when compounded forward *instantaneously* yields the cumulative return derived from the actual periodic returns.

- The continuous return is equal to the natural logarithm of the periodic return's wealth relative.

- The base of the natural logarithm *e*, which equals 2.718282, is the limit of 1 invested at a 100% rate of return, compounded continuously for one period.

- When raised to a power equal to the continuous return, *e* produces a value equal to 1 plus the periodic return, which is the wealth relative.

- An investment that may either increase or decrease by specified percentages, when repeated over many periods or divided into smaller and smaller periods, produces a distribution of cumulative returns whose corresponding continuous returns are normally distributed.

- The entire normal distribution can be inferred from just two values, its mean and its variance, which is usually expressed as its square root, the standard deviation.

- Finally, we are able to characterize an investment's riskiness from its mean and standard deviation of continuous returns because the normal distribution permits us to map these values onto probability estimates of achieving or failing to achieve various outcomes.

If you are comfortable with these concepts you qualify as a dilequant[5] and should have no trouble unraveling the puzzles of finance.

---

[5] One who dabbles in quantitative methods.

GLOSSARY

American option. An option that can be exercised at expiration or any time prior to expiration, as opposed to a European option, which can only be exercised at expiration. The labels, American and European, were given by Paul A. Samuelson. See also *option, European option.*

Annualization. Translation of a rate of return covering less than one year or more than one year into an equivalent annual rate.

Annualized return. The rate of return that would occur on average per year given a cumulative return covering more than one year or less than one year. See also *constant rate of return, geometric average return.*

Arithmetic average. The sum of a series of values divided by the number of values in the series. See also *mean.*

Arithmetic Brownian motion. A stochastic process that describes the dispersion of continuous returns through time. See also *Brownian motion, geometric Brownian motion.*

Bell curve. Another name for a normal distribution because its shape resembles the curvature of a bell. See also *normal distribution.*

Beta. A measure of an asset or portfolio's relative volatility with a reference portfolio. It is estimated as the slope of a regression line relating an asset or portfolio's excess return over the riskless return to a reference portfolio's excess return over the riskless return. Within the context of the Capital Asset Pricing Model, beta when squared and multiplied by the market's variance, represents an asset or portfolio's nondiversiable risk. See also *Capital Asset Pricing Model, diversifiable risk, nondiversifiable risk, variance.*

Binomial process. A representation of a return generating process in which an asset's value can either increase by a specified amount with a given probability or decrease by a specified amount with one minus the probability of the increase in a single period from all immediate prior values. The ending distribution of values from a binomial process will converge to a normal or lognormal distribution, as the number of periods becomes large.

Black-Scholes formula. A formula that gives the fair value of an option based on five inputs: the price of the underlying asset, the exercise price, the riskless interest rate, the time remaining to expiration, and the volatility of the underlying asset's return. It is the solution to a partial differential equation based on a neutral hedge that combines offsetting exposures to an option and its underlying asset.

Bootstrapping. A procedure by which new samples are generated from an original data set by randomly selecting observations with replacement from the original data. See also *Monte Carlo simulation.*

Brownian motion. A stochastic process that is normally distributed with an average change equal to zero and a variance that increases proportionally with the passage of time. The term is named after Robert Brown, a nineteenth-century Scottish botanist who observed and recorded the dispersion of particles within pollen grains suspended in water after colliding with water molecules. See also *arithmetic Brownian motion, geometric Brownian motion, lognormal distribution, normal distribution, stochastic process.*

Call option. An option that grants its owner the right but not the obligation to purchase an underlying asset at a previously agreed upon price at or up to a specified future date (American) or only at a specified future date (European). See also *American option, European option, option, put option.*

Capital Asset Pricing Model (CAPM). A theory of market equilibrium which partitions risk into two sources: that caused by changes in the market portfolio, which cannot be diversified away, and that caused by nonmarket factors, which can be diversified away. An asset's nondiversifiable risk is equal to its beta squared multiplied by the market portfolio's variance. The CAPM implies that investors should incur only nondiversiable risk because they are not compensated for bearing diversifiable risk. The CAPM was developed simultaneously and independently by John Lintner, Jan Mossin, William Sharpe, and Jack Treynor. See also *beta, diversiable risk, nondiversifiable risk, variance.*

Central limit theorem. The principle that the distribution of the sum or average of independent random variables, which are not necessarily individually normally distributed, will approach a normal distribution as the number of variables increases. See also *normal distribution, random variable.*

Certainty equivalent. A risky gamble or investment that conveys the same amount of expected utility as the utility associated with a certain outcome. See also *expected utility.*

Change of variables. A transformation that converts a partial differential equation into an ordinary differential equation, which is easier to solve analytically. See also *ordinary differential equation, partial differential equation.*

Cobb-Douglas utility function. A utility function in which satisfaction or happiness derived from consumption of various goods or services is proportional to the fraction of income spent on each good or service. See also *expected utility, utility function.*

Constant rate of return. The rate of return, that were it to occur on average annually, would produce the cumulative return that actually occurred. See also *annualized return, cumulative return, expected return, geometric average return.*

Constant relative risk aversion. A measure of risk aversion which holds that investors prefer to maintain the same proportion of their wealth in risky assets as their wealth grows. See also *log-wealth utility function.*

Contingent claim. A claim that depends on the occurrence of a previously agreed upon outcome. For example, a call option is a contingent claim because its owner has a claim on the underlying asset should its value exceed the exercise price at maturity. See also *option.*

Continuous return. The rate of return, which if compounded continuously or instantaneously, would generate the corresponding periodic return. It is equal to the natural logarithm of the quantity, one plus the periodic return. See also *e, natural logarithm, periodic return.*

Covariance. A measure of the co-movement of the returns of two assets. It is equal to the correlation between the two assets' returns times the first asset's standard deviation times the second asset's standard deviation. Combinations of assets that have low covariances are desirable because they offer greater diversification. See also *correlation, standard deviation, variance.*

Covered interest arbitrage. The principle that one cannot borrow in a low interest country, convert to the currency of a high interest rate country, lend in the high interest rate country, hedge the currency risk of the loan, and generate a profit. The absence of arbitrage profits from these transactions ensures that the forward exchange rate will equal the spot exchange rate multiplied by the ratio of one plus the domestic interest rate to one plus the foreign interest rate. See also *forward exchange rate, spot exchange rate, uncovered interest arbitrage.*

Cumulative probability. The sum of all the probabilities of potential outcomes between two points. See also *frequency distribution, histogram, normal distribution.*

Cumulative return. The unannualized return that is equal to the product of the quantities, one plus the periodic returns, minus one, or equivalently, the ending value divided by the beginning value minus one, assuming reinvestment of income and controlling for contributions and disbursements. See also *annualized return, periodic return.*

Currency cross rate. The implied exchange rate between two currencies that is derived from their respective exchange rates with a third currency. If the exchange rate between the U.S. dollar and the euro equals 1.0500 dollars per euro, and the U.S. dollar's exchange rate with the British pound equals 1.6000 dollars per pound, the cross rate between the euro and the pound equals 1.5238 euros per pound (1.6000/1.0500) or 0.6523 pounds per euro (1.0500/1.6000).

Differential equation. An equation that contains one or more derivative terms. Derivative terms measure how much a particular variable changes given a vanishingly small change in another variable. See also *ordinary differential equation, partial differential equation.*

Discontinuous utility function. A utility function that is kinked because, for a small change in wealth at a particular threshold, utility changes abruptly rather than smoothly. See also *constant relative risk aversion, log-wealth utility function, utility function.*

Discount rate. The interest rate that is used to equate future cash flows to a present value. See also *discounted expected value, present value.*

Discounted expected value. The present value of an expected future value that is derived by dividing all possible future values by the quantity, one plus the discount rate, and then calculating the expected value of these discounted values. See also *discount rate, expected value, present value.*

Diversifiable risk.   Risk that is specific to an asset and thus not associated with market risk. In an efficient market investors should not bear diversifiable risk because it is not rewarded. See also *beta, Capital Asset Pricing Model, nondiversiable risk.*

e.   The base of the natural logarithm and the limit of the function $(1+1/n)^n$. To four decimal places, it equals 2.7183. When e is raised to the power of a continuous return, it is equal to one plus the periodic return. See also *continuous return, natural logarithm, periodic return.*

Efficient frontier.   A continuum of portfolios plotted in dimensions of expected return and standard deviation that offer the highest expected return for a given level of risk or the lowest risk for a given expected return. See also *expected return, separation theorem, standard deviation.*

European option.   An option that can be exercised only at expiration, as opposed to an American option, which can be exercised at expiration or any time up to expiration. The labels, American and European, were given by Paul A. Samuelson. See also *option, American option.*

Excess return.   That part of return that exceeds the riskless return.

Exercise price.   The price for the underlying asset that determines whether or not an option is in the money (has value) at expiration. The underlying asset's price must exceed the exercise price for a call option to have value, whereas it must be below the exercise price for a put option to have value. Also called strike price or striking price. See also *call option, option, strike price, put option.*

Expected return. The average or probability weighted value of all possible returns. The process of compounding causes the expected return to exceed the median return. Thus there is less than a 50% chance of exceeding the expected return. See also *arithmetic average, geometric average return, lognormal distribution, mean, skewness.*

Expected utility. The average or probability weighted utility or measure of satisfaction associated with all possible wealth or consumption levels. See also *expected value, utility function.*

Expected value. The average or probability weighted value of all possible wealth values. It is equal to the initial value compounded forward at the expected return, which if based on historical returns, equals the arithmetic average return. See also *expected return.*

Financial engineering. The practice of applying financial theory and quantitative methods to solve financial problems and to manage financial risk.

First passage time problem. A class of problems that address the likelihood of a value penetrating a threshold at any time during a specified time horizon.

Forward exchange rate. A previously agreed upon rate at which currencies are exchanged at a specified future date. See also *covered interest arbitrage, spot exchange rate, uncovered interest arbitrage.*

Frequency distribution. A discrete probability distribution usually represented by a bar chart called a histogram that shows the percentage of observations contained within a specified interval. See also *histogram, normal distribution.*

Generalized Weiner process. A mathematical model of Brownian motion that allows for a drift in the random variable. See also *Brownian motion, Weiner process.*

Geometric average return. The average annual return that, when compounded forward, converts an initial value to an ending value. It is equal to the product of the quantities, one plus the annual periodic returns, raised to the power, one over the number of periodic returns, less one. When based on historical returns, an initial value compounded forward at the geometric average return yields the median value. The natural logarithm of the quantity, one plus the geometric average return, equals the continuous return. Also called annualized return or constant rate of return. See also *annualized return, constant rate of return, continuous return, expected return, expected value, median, natural logarithm.*

Geometric Brownian motion. A stochastic process that describes the dispersion of periodic returns through time. See *arithmetic Brownian motion, Brownian motion.*

Heat exchange equation. An equation that measures heat migration through a substance such as a metal rod. Its solution, developed by Albert Einstein in 1905, provides an important linkage in the discovery of the Black-Scholes formula.

Histogram. A bar chart representing a discrete probability distribution that shows the percentage of observations contained within specified intervals. Also called a frequency distribution. See also *frequency distribution, normal distribution.*

Independent and identically distributed (iid). A condition in which successive draws from a population are independent of one another and generated from the same underlying distribution, implying that the parameters of an iid distribution are constant across all draws. See also *random variable.*

Investment. A resource that is not consumed but rather held to generate income and/or capital gains.

Jensen's inequality. The mathematical fact that the expected value of a reciprocal is greater than the reciprocal of the expected value. See also *Siegel's paradox*.

Law of large numbers. The principle that as a sample becomes large, measures of its central tendency and dispersion become more accurate. See also *central limit theorem, time diversification*.

Law of one price. The economic principle that assets with identical cash flows should be priced the same. See also *MM invariance propositions*.

Logarithm. The power to which a base must be raised to yield a particular number. For example, the logarithm of 100 to the base 10 equals 2, because 10^2 equals 100. Prior to the advent of calculators, logarithms were convenient because, with an implement called a slide rule, one could multiply numbers by adding their logarithms. See also *e, natural logarithm*.

Lognormal distribution. A distribution of periodic returns or cumulative values that is positively skewed as a result of compounding. Compared to a normal distribution, which is symmetric, a lognormal distribution has a longer right tail than left tail and an average value that exceeds the median value. A lognormal distribution of periodic returns corresponds to a normal distribution of their continuous counterparts. See also *normal distribution, skewness*.

Log-wealth utility function. A concave utility function that assumes utility is equal to the logarithm of wealth. It is one of a family of utility functions that assume investors have constant relative risk aversion. For investors with a log-wealth utility function, as wealth increases, its utility also increases but at a diminishing rate. See also *constant relative risk aversion, natural logarithm, utility function*.

Mean. The arithmetic average. See also *arithmetic average.*

Mean aversion. The tendency of an above average return to be followed by another above average return and a below average return to be followed by another below average return, resulting in a higher incidence of trends than would be expected from a random process. See also *mean reversion, random variable.*

Mean reversion. The tendency of an above average return to be followed by a below average return and a below average return to be followed by an above return, resulting in a higher incidence of reversals than would be expected from a random process. See also *mean aversion, random variable.*

Measure of central tendency. A statistic used to summarize a set of data. Together with measures of dispersion, it allows one to assess the confidence with which an outcome will exceed or fall short of a particular value. Measures of central tendency include the mean, which is the average value, the median, which is the middle value, and the mode, which is the most common value. See also *mean, measure of dispersion, median, mode.*

Measure of dispersion. A statistic used to summarize the variation in a set of data. Together with measures of central tendency, it allows one to assess the confidence with which an outcome will exceed or fall short of a particular value. Measures of dispersion include mean absolute deviation, standard deviation and variance. See also *measure of central tendency, standard deviation, variance.*

Median. The middle value of a set of data. Based on historical returns, an initial value compounded forward at the geometric average return yields the median ending value. See also *geometric average return, mean, measure of central tendency, mode.*

MM invariance propositions. The principles put forth by Franco Modigliani and Merton Miller that the value of a firm is invariant to its capital structure and dividend policy, because investors can individually engage in arbitrage to offset capital structure, and because dividend payments and share repurchases are substitutes. Their insights about arbitrage paved the way for the discovery of the Black-Scholes formula. See also *law of one price*.

Mode. The most common value of a set of data. See also *mean, measure of central tendency, median*.

Monte Carlo simulation. A process used to simulate the performance of an investment strategy by randomly selecting returns from an underlying theoretical distribution such as a normal or lognormal distribution and subjecting the investment strategy to these randomly selected returns. It is used to assess path dependent investment strategies. See also *bootstrapping, lognormal distribution, normal distribution, path dependency, random variable*.

Natural logarithm. The continuous return to which e, 2.7183, must be raised to yield one plus the corresponding periodic return. For example, e raised to the power 0.0953 gives 1.1000, which equals one plus the periodic return of 0.1000. It follows, therefore, the natural logarithm of the quantity, one plus the periodic return yields the corresponding continuous return. See also *continuous return, e, natural logarithm, periodic return*.

Nondiversifiable risk. Risk that is associated with variation in the return of the market portfolio. It is equal to beta squared times the market's variance. In an efficient market, investors should only bear nondiversiable risk, because unlike diversiable risk, it is rewarded. See also *beta, Capital Asset Pricing Model, diversifiable risk*.

Normal deviate. The number of standard deviation units a particular value is away from the mean under a normal distribution. It is equal to the difference between the value of interest and the mean, divided by the standard deviation. A normal distribution converts a normal deviate into the corresponding area under a normal distribution by re-scaling the distribution to have a mean of zero and a standard deviation of one. Also called standardized variable. See also *normal distribution, standardized variable.*

Normal distribution. A continuous probability distribution that often arises from the summation of a large number of random variables. It has the convenient property that its mean, median, and mode are all equal. Also, approximately 68% of its area falls within a range of the mean plus and minus one standard deviation, and approximately 95% of its area falls within a range of the mean plus and minus two standard deviations. See also *central limit theorem, frequency distribution, lognormal distribution.*

Option. A contract that grants its owner the right, but not the obligation, to purchase (call option) or sell (put option) an underlying asset at a pre-established price for a specified period of time. See also *American option, Black-Scholes formula, call option, European option, put option.*

Ordinary differential equation. A differential equation that contains the derivatives of a single variable. See also *differential equation, partial differential equation.*

Partial differential equation. A differential equation that contains the derivatives of two or more variables. See also *differential equation, ordinary differential equation.*

Path dependency. A condition in which the terminal value of an investment strategy depends on the particular sequence of returns and not just the average return. See also *bootstrapping, Monte Carlo simulation.*

Periodic return. The income produced by an investment plus its change in price over a specified period, all divided by its price at the beginning of the period. See also *continuous return, cumulative return.*

Preference dependent. An approach to valuation in which the value of an asset depends on investors' particular preferences with respect to risk. See also *preference free, risk neutral.*

Preference free. An approach to valuation in which the value of an asset is invariant to investors' particular preferences with respect to risk. Instead it is derived by the absence of arbitrage. See also *preference dependent, risk neutral.*

Present value. The value today of a future cash flow or sequence of cash flows that is derived by discounting them by a discount factor. See also *discount rate.*

Purchasing power parity. The principle that exchange rates adjust so that the cost of similar goods and services remains the same in all countries, which implies that changes in currency exchange rates reflect relative inflation. Violations of purchasing power parity occur and may persist for extended periods because consumer preferences differ from country to country and because there are impediments to trade. In the long run, however, it is reasonable to expect that arbitrage of goods and services will force exchange rates and prices to converge. See also *law of one price.*

Put option. An option that grants its owner the right, but not the obligation, to sell an underlying asset at a previously agreed upon price at or up to a specified future date (American) or only at a specified future date (European). See also *American option, call option, European option, option.*

Random variable. A variable that can take on a variety of uncertain values. For example, an asset's value at a future date is a random variable as is the value resulting from the toss of a die. See also *random walk.*

Random walk. A stochastic process in which future values of a random variable are unrelated to its current value. Variables that are believed to follow a random walk are said to be independent and identically distributed. See also *independent and identically distributed, random variable, stochastic process.*

Relative frequency. The percentage of observations from a sample that falls within a specified interval. See also *frequency distribution, histogram.*

Risk. The likelihood of experiencing an unpleasant outcome such as a significant loss or failure to achieve an expected gain. Investment risk is typically construed as uncertainty, and it is measured by the standard deviation or variance of an expected return. See also *standard deviation, variance.*

Risk neutral valuation. A valuation method, often used to value options, that discounts the expected terminal value of an asset by the riskless return, even though the expected return of the asset is different from the riskless return. See also *Black-Scholes formula, constant relative risk aversion, risk neutrality.*

Risk neutrality. The notion that an investor is indifferent between an uncertain outcome and a certain outcome as long as they have the same expected return. See also *certainty equivalent, risk, risk neutral valuation.*

Separation theorem. The principle, put forth by James Tobin, that the investment process can be separated into two distinct steps, (1) the choice of a unique optimal portfolio along the efficient frontier, and (2) the decision to combine this portfolio with a riskless investment. See also *Capital Asset Pricing Model, efficient frontier.*

Sharpe ratio. An asset or portfolio's expected return in excess of the riskless return, all divided by its standard deviation. It is used to compare mutually independent investment alternatives. See also *beta, Capital Asset Pricing Model, standard deviation.*

Siegel's paradox. A variation of Jensen's inequality applied to currency exchange rates. It refers to the mathematical fact that the expected value of the reciprocal of an exchange rate is greater then the reciprocal of the expected value of the exchange rate. It follows from Siegel's paradox that a given percentage increase in an exchange rate from the perspective of one base currency corresponds to a decrease of smaller magnitude from the perspective of the other base currency. See also *Jensen's inequality.*

Skewness. Asymmetry in a distribution. For example, a lognormal distribution is positively skewed, which means that the right tail extends further to the right than the left tail extends to the left. As a consequence, the mean of the distribution exceeds its median. See also *lognormal distribution, mean, median.*

Spot exchange rate. The rate at which currencies are exchanged at the present time as opposed to a future date. See also *covered interest arbitrage, forward exchange rate, uncovered interest arbitrage.*

Standard deviation. A measure of dispersion that is commonly used to measure an asset's riskiness. It is equal to the square root of the average of the squared deviations from the mean, and it is the square root of the variance. Approximately 68% of the observations under a normal distribution fall within the mean plus and minus one standard deviation. See also *measure of dispersion, normal distribution, variance.*

Standardized variable. The number of standard deviation units a particular value is away from the mean under a normal distribution. It is equal to the difference between the value of interest and the mean, divided by the standard deviation. A normal distribution converts a standardized variable into the corresponding area under a normal distribution by re-scaling the distribution to have a mean of zero and a standard deviation of one. Also called normal deviate. See also *normal deviate, normal distribution.*

Stochastic process. A process in which a random variable can take on a variety of uncertain future values that are unrelated to its current value, as opposed to a deterministic process in which future values are determined by the current value. See also *generalized Weiner process, random variable, random walk, Weiner process.*

Strike price. The price for the underlying asset that determines whether or not an option is in the money (has value) at expiration. The underlying asset's price must exceed the strike price for a call option to have value, whereas it must be below the strike price for a put option to have value. Also called exercise price or striking price. See also *call option, option, put option.*

Striking price. See *strike price.*

Time diversification. The notion that above average returns tend to offset below average returns over long time horizons. It does not follow, however, that time reduces risk. Although the likelihood of a loss decreases with time for investments with positive expected returns, the potential magnitude of a loss increases with time. See also *law of large numbers.*

Unbiased estimate. An estimate that is the mean of the distribution of future values. See also *uncovered interest arbitrage.*

Uncovered interest arbitrage. The notion that one cannot borrow in a low interest rate country, convert to the currency of a high interest rate country, lend in the high interest rate country, and generate a profit. The gains that occur in some periods from these transactions are offset by losses in other periods, so that the average gain is zero. If uncovered interest arbitrage holds, the expected return of a currency forward contract is 0%. Siegel's paradox guarantees that uncovered interest arbitrage cannot hold simultaneously from the perspective of both sides of an exchange rate. See also *covered interest arbitrage, forward exchange rate, Siegel's paradox, spot exchange rate.*

Uniform distribution. A probability distribution for which there is an equal probability for all of the possible values of a random variable. For example, the distribution of the values from the toss of a single die has a uniform distribution. See also *normal distribution*.

Utility function. The relationship between varying levels of wealth or consumption of goods and services and the happiness or satisfaction imparted by the different wealth and consumption levels. A commonly invoked utility function for economic modeling is the log-wealth utility function, which implies that utility increases at a decreasing rate as wealth increases. See also *Cobb-Douglas utility function, constant relative risk aversion, discontinuous utility function, log-wealth utility function*.

Variance. A measure of dispersion used to characterize an asset's riskiness. It is equal to the average of the squared deviations from the mean, and its square root is the standard deviation. See also *measure of dispersion, standard deviation*.

Wealth relative. A value equal to one plus a periodic rate of return. The geometric average return is computed by taking the product of wealth relatives, raising this product to the power, one divided by the number of wealth relatives, and subtracting one. The continuous return is computed as the natural logarithm of the wealth relative. See also *continuous return, geometric average return, periodic return*.

Weiner process. A mathematical model of Brownian motion based on four assumptions: (1) there exists a normally distributed random variable for any time interval greater than zero; (2) prior to the passage of time the value of this random variable is zero; (3) at all future times the expected value of this random variable is zero; and (4) the change in the value of the random variable is independent from interval to interval. See also *Brownian motion, generalized Weiner process*.

INDEX